AMAZING
Furniture Makeovers

Easy DIY Projects to Transform Thrifted Finds into Beautiful Custom Pieces

JEN CRIDER

Founder of Girl in the Garage

PAGE STREET
PUBLISHING CO.

PAGE STREET
PUBLISHING CO.

Copyright © 2019 Jen Crider

First published in 2019 by

Page Street Publishing Co.

27 Congress Street, Suite 105

Salem, MA 01970

www.pagestreetpublishing.com

Distributed by Macmillan, sales in Canada by The Canadian Manda Group.

23 22 21 20 19   1 2 3 4 5

ISBN-13: 978-1-62414-795-1

ISBN-10: 1-62414-795-X

Library of Congress Control Number: 2019931082

Cover and book design by Rosie Stewart for Page Street Publishing Co.
Photography by Jen Crider

Printed and bound in the United States

DEDICATION

To my husband Scott, and our children Xander, Phoenix, and Emerson

And to my mother, Susan

BICYCLE

THE MOST COMPREHENSIVE CYCLING CATALOGUE FREE

POPE MFG CO., 79 FRANKLIN ST., BOSTON.

Contents

Suitcase Dresser (page 143), Bicycle Armoire (page 99)

Introduction

Hello, lovely. I have a feeling we're going to become good friends. Since you're reading this book right now, we probably have a lot in common. Does your heart skip a beat when you're thrifting and you score an awesome piece for a great price? Could you spend hours perusing DIY blogs and Pinterest for ideas and inspiration? Do you slam on the brakes when you spy a discarded antique dresser by the side of the road? Do you spend your free time cleaning, prepping, and refinishing old furniture to make it ready to be loved and treasured again?

I've been updating furniture and sharing tutorials online since 2012, and it never gets boring. Every piece is different and special in its own way and gets its own unique style of makeover. On occasion I buy some pretty ugly pieces that are real fixer-uppers, but I've been told I have a knack for seeing potential where others can't.

Whether you're new to refinishing furniture or you've been doing it for years, I hope this book gives you confidence to overcome your fears, knowledge to tackle projects without hesitation, and fresh inspiration to incorporate into your own creative projects. I'm honored that you've chosen this book to read, and I am so excited to be on this journey with you!

Jen

—Jen, aka Girl in the Garage®

P.S. My handsome, handy husband (aka "Guy in the Garage") sometimes helps with my projects, especially when a piece needs to be stained or wood needs to be cut. So, if you see manly hands in some of the photos, that's why!

Vintage Soda Pop Machine (page 147)

Tips for Buying Furniture

Not All Furniture Is Created Equal

If you want to spend your time on well-made pieces that will last, stay away from plasticky furniture that is mass-produced and sold for cheap at big chain stores. I usually only work on antique or vintage pieces that are real wood or laminate, like mid-century modern furniture. Check the joints and look for stamps or other maker's marks.

Avoid These Issues

If you don't have much experience in dealing with major repairs, avoid pieces with water damage (water rings can be sanded away, but bubbled up veneer is much harder to deal with), pieces that are already painted (be prepared for lots of sanding and stripping—and check for lead paint with a lead paint test kit before you buy), chairs with broken or cracked legs, and any pieces that need repairs that are beyond your skill level. If you're in doubt, skip it.

Popular Styles for Updating and Reselling

If you're planning on refinishing furniture to sell, stick with pieces that have storage (with drawers or doors) such as dressers, buffets, sideboards, cabinets, nightstands, desks, and chests. Also popular are antiques with a lot of intricate details and mid-century pieces with clean lines. Finally, seek out pieces with flat fronts for creative finishes like stenciling, image transfers, decoupage, and upholstery tack designs.

Bienvenue Bench (page 89), Singer Sewing Table to Planked Desk (page 163)

Products and Tools

Having the right tools and using the best products for the task can make all the difference in how your furniture makeover turns out. Here are some recommendations for what I prefer to use. (Learn some Tips for Repairs and Prep on page 182.)

1. First, always read and follow the directions when using any tool or product. For example, wear safety goggles, gloves, a mask, etc., depending on what you're doing. You should work outside or in a well-ventilated area if there will be fumes or if you'll be making a big mess.

2. I mostly use Annie Sloan Chalk Paint® for my makeovers. It works especially well when you want to distress a piece and achieve a matte finish. It also cleans up quite easily if you're a messy painter like me! I also like Fusion™ Mineral Paint for a sleek, smooth finish when I don't plan to distress. Plus, it doesn't require a topcoat.

3. I prefer Annie Sloan's wax as a topcoat because it's purposely meant to work well with Chalk Paint and because it will never yellow over paint like many others do. However, it's not meant for pieces that will be exposed to heat or any type of weather, and it has a total cure time of about 30 days. I apply wax to small areas (like a chair or small table) with a lint-free cloth, and to larger areas with a wax brush. Refer to the directions on the can for the best possible results.

4. For staining, I prefer Minwax® stain and then Rust-Oleum Varathane® polyurethane as a topcoat. Applying a pre-stain conditioner first helps to even out the color of the stain (it's kind of like primer, but for stain).

Rustic Stenciled Dresser (page 29)

5. I have brushes of all sizes that I use for painting and dedicated ones I use just for primer, stain, wax, and poly. My go-to paintbrushes are Purdy®, and I use Annie Sloan's wax brushes for waxing large pieces. You won't be sorry for buying good-quality brushes that, with proper care, will last for years.

6. A Kreg Jig® kit is great for making pocket holes (holes drilled at an angle to accommodate screws) when woodworking.

7. An air compressor and staple gun are definitely helpful for big upholstery projects.

8. A chop/miter saw is ideal for making clean cuts and angles on smaller pieces of wood. It has a mounted blade that you pull down onto the wood.

9. A table saw makes almost any cut, especially long straight cuts. You guide the wood through the blade that protrudes from the cutting table. It's very powerful but also potentially more dangerous than a chop saw.

Start with Simple:
WORKING WITH PAINT AND STAIN

A new can of paint holds so many possibilities—refresh a beloved family heirloom, update a thrifted dresser for a new baby's nursery, or give your old bedroom set a facelift before passing it on to another family member. Maybe even pursue your passion to start a furniture refinishing business.

There are countless ways to update furniture, and it's easy to feel overwhelmed with all the possibilities and unsure about where to start. Don't worry, friend—we're going to start with simple. You'll learn the basics about working with paint, stain, and wax to achieve a beautiful finish without making things complicated. When you're ready, you can explore the other creative techniques presented in later chapters as you grow in confidence, knowledge, and experience.

In this chapter, you'll hardly recognize a Goodwill buffet after just one coat of paint and dark wax (page 15) and witness an ugly-duckling dresser transform into a beauty with a newly stained top and painted bottom (page 21). Remember to look for tips in every project so you can avoid mistakes and ensure your makeovers go more smoothly. Are you ready? Let's get started!

Moody Blue Buffet (page 15), Pretty in Pink and Walnut (page 21)

Moody Blue Buffet

Antique buffets like this are popular not only for dining rooms but also as repurposed TV stands in living rooms or bedrooms. They're not too hard to find secondhand and can be easily refreshed with new paint. You could stick with a basic neutral—but why not have some fun and choose an unexpected color? In this tutorial, you'll see how one color of paint and dark wax turned this boring brown buffet into a bold blue beauty.

Supplies

Staple remover

Wood filler (I used Elmer's ProBond® wood filler)

Small scraper

220-grit sandpaper

Scraper

Tape measure

¼" (6-mm) wood sheet

Table saw (or have wood cut at the hardware store)

Safety glasses and hearing protection

Wood glue or DAP® adhesive caulk

Clamps

Hammer

Small nails (1" [2.5 cm] or shorter)

Blue paint (I used Annie Sloan Chalk Paint® in Napoleonic Blue)

Paintbrush

Brown furniture wax (I used Annie Sloan's dark brown wax)

Lint-free cloths

New knobs or pulls

Before

1. Start by cleaning your piece, especially if it's been in your garage for a couple of years. Ahem. Refer to page 182 for helpful tips on making repairs and prepping your piece for a makeover.

2. Then remove any old dishcloths that were stapled inside the drawers.

3. This vintage piece had dents, scratches, some chipping veneer, and beautiful rustic wood grain on top. I opted to fill some of the big imperfections with a scraper and wood filler and leave some as part of its character and history.

4. Let the wood filler dry for 20 to 30 minutes, depending on how wide and deep the area is, then lightly sand over the filled areas for smoothness.

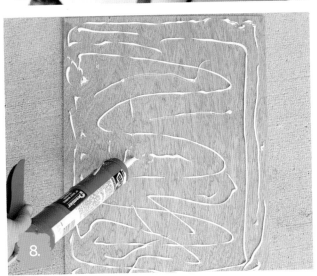

5. Behind the two doors, it was partially painted and there were weird clumps stuck to the bottom. I used a scraper and 220-grit sandpaper to smooth over those areas.

6. Both sides of the buffet had large chunks of veneer missing.

7. Since those areas were inset anyway, Guy in the Garage measured and cut thin panels of wood to fit over both sides.

8. Spread wood glue all over the panel. I used adhesive caulk because it was available nearby.

9. Insert the new panel over the inset area, pressing firmly. Use clamps to hold it in place and let it dry.

10. Hammer a small nail near each corner to keep it more secure. I used 1-inch (2.5-cm) nails, but you should choose nails that are short enough not to poke through to the inside of your piece.

11. Next, paint the buffet with approximately two coats of blue paint. I almost flipped the first time I used this color blue—it looks so electric when it's still wet!

12. Here you can see the difference between when the paint is dry on top and when it's still wet. Thankfully it tones down a lot.

13. Sand and paint the drawers also. If the drawers had been in better shape, I wouldn't have painted them. But it looked like there was felt glued down sometime before the dishcloths were stapled on.

Give everything 2 to 3 coats of paint as needed, letting the paint dry for about 20 to 30 minutes between coats. Then lightly sand it, focusing more on the edges and details first before moving to random smaller areas on the buffet for a naturally distressed look. You want it to look like it has gently weathered over time.

14. Protect the buffet with a dark brown wax topcoat. Wipe it on with a lint-free cloth, working it into the grooves and details. Wipe away the excess with another cloth. The brown tones down the blue even more and helps give it that rustic finish we're going for. In this photo, the left side has no wax and the right side has the dark wax. The wax should feel dry to the touch within 24 hours. However, the full cure time for wax is about 30 days, so be gentle with your piece for the first month or so.

15. Add new hardware, such as glass knobs like these to class it up, or maybe something in bronze to keep everything dark and consistent.

Pretty in Pink and Walnut

I must confess, this antique dresser sat buried in my storage unit for several years after I scored it for only nine dollars at a yard sale. Even though it needed quite a bit of work, who could resist a deal like that? Finally, she stands proud with a sweet two-tone look—a newly stained top and perfectly pink bottom. In this project, you'll learn how to confidently tackle exterior problems so you can dig that damaged antique out of the back of *your* garage.

Supplies

Wide scraper

Random orbit sander

Safety glasses and face mask for protection

¼" (6-mm) plywood paneling

Table saw (or have the wood cut at the hardware store)

Wood glue or DAP® adhesive caulk

Clamps

Hammer

Small nails (1" [2.5 cm] or shorter)

Wood filler (I used Elmer's ProBond® wood filler)

Small scraper

220-grit sandpaper

Minwax® Pre-Stain Wood Conditioner

Lint-free cloths

Gloves

Minwax® Wood Finish Stain in Special Walnut

Rust-Oleum Varathane® matte polyurethane

Wide brush for polyurethane

Brown paint (I used Annie Sloan Chalk Paint® in Honfleur)

Paintbrushes

Pink paint (I used Annie Sloan Chalk Paint® in Scandinavian Pink)

Small detail paintbrush

320-grit sandpaper

Furniture wax (I used Annie Sloan's clear wax)

Wax brush

New knobs or pulls

Before

1. This dresser was a real beauty about 100 years or so ago.

2. Unfortunately, the top was badly damaged and there were nicks and scratches everywhere.

3. The veneer on top was so brittle that it came off easily with a scraper and a little bit of effort. If your veneer is tough to remove, lay a damp hot towel on top for several hours to soften the veneer glue, and then pry it off with a scraper. Refer to page 182 for helpful tips on making repairs and prepping your piece for a makeover.

4. Sand the top smooth with a random orbit sander.

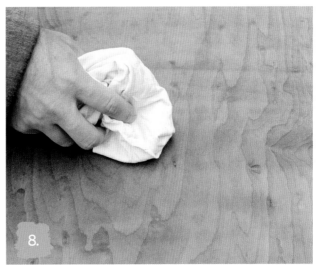

5. Just like in the Moody Blue Buffet makeover (page 15), both sides of this dresser had big chunks of chipping veneer. If you have the same problem, cut two panels to fit within the inset areas. Apply wood glue or adhesive caulk all over the "less pretty" side of the panels.

6. Press the panels into place and leave them clamped for several hours. Hammer a nail near each corner to keep it more secure. I used 1-inch (2.5-cm) nails, but you should choose nails that are short enough not to poke through to the inside of your piece.

7. Carefully fill small chips and gouges with wood filler and a scraper. After about 20 to 30 minutes, make sure it's dry and then lightly sand the area smooth with 220-grit sandpaper.

8. Wipe pre-stain wood conditioner on the top of the dresser with a lint-free cloth. The conditioner helps prevent blotchiness and gives the stain a more even finish.

9. Next, put on work gloves and slowly apply the stain in long, even strokes with a lint-free cloth. Press the stain into the wood grain. Once the entire surface has been covered, wipe the excess stain away with a clean cloth and let it dry for at least 30 minutes. This dresser top received three coats of Special Walnut stain.

10. Protect the stained top by applying a polyurethane topcoat with a wide brush. Never shake the can, just gently stir it. You do not want bubbles in your poly! Work in long strokes, about half the length of the top. Make sure you have even coverage, and keep an extra cloth nearby to wipe away drips near the edges. Let the poly dry. The dry time varies depending on your temperature and humidity. Check it after 30 minutes to see if it looks dry enough for another coat of poly. Apply 2 to 3 more coats of poly. The top will be dry enough for light usage after 24 hours.

11. Paint the unfinished wood sides brown so the base color will be consistent everywhere once you paint over it.

12. Paint the body and drawers in a fun color like pink. You may need 2 to 3 coats for even coverage.

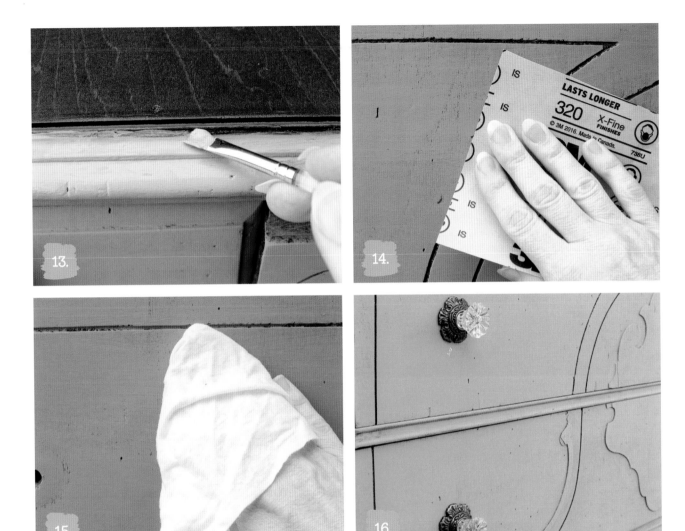

13. Use a small detail brush to paint near the stained top.

14. Lightly sand over the edges, curves and details with 320-grit sandpaper for a naturally distressed finish. You want the wood to peek through from underneath the paint, but don't overdo it or it won't look very natural.

15. Brush clear wax over the painted areas for protection. Work in small sections and wipe away the excess wax with a lint-free cloth. The full cure time for wax is about 30 days, so be gentle with it for the first month or so.

16. Lastly, add some bling with fancy new knobs so this lovely lady can really shine!

Painted Pattern
TECHNIQUES

An easy way to make plain furniture fabulous is with painted patterns. Stencils, stripes, and even random shapes and unexpected tools from around your home can create custom designs to make your pieces unique.

Use painted patterns on the fronts of drawers, the sides of dressers, the tops of tables, the back of bookcases, and even the insides of drawers for an unexpected surprise. You can mix patterns, like stripes and a stencil, for a special look.

The products you're using can make a difference in how your project turns out. For stencils, I have several from Royal Design Studio Stencils online and from various sellers on Etsy as well. Just read some reviews first to make sure the stencils are made from good-quality materials. For stripes, I prefer to use FrogTape® Delicate Surface yellow painter's tape. If you're using it over a recently painted surface, just be sure to give the area plenty of time to dry completely before applying the tape.

In this chapter, you'll find out how to paint stenciled designs and polka dots for a whimsical look (page 29), paint stripes without the hassle of measuring (page 35), and even create your own batik-inspired design with dots from a pencil eraser (page 41).

Striped Chateau Dresser (page 35), Batik-Inspired MCM Nightstand (page 41)

Rustic Stenciled Dresser

If furniture could talk, I'm sure this piece would tell some incredible stories from its lifetime. Even though the finish was a bit dated, the late-1800s Knapp joints, primitive nails, and keyholes have such rustic charm. And the drawers all slid smoothly, which is a rare find in such an aged piece!

I wanted to update this dresser in a way that would enhance its charm and add a touch of whimsy. This makeover will demonstrate how to refresh a very old antique while keeping its original character.

Supplies

Wood filler (I used Elmer's ProBond® wood filler)

Small scraper

220-grit sandpaper

Gray paint (I used Annie Sloan Chalk Paint® in Paris Grey)

Paintbrushes

320-grit sandpaper

Lint-free cloths

Painter's tape

Stencil (I used Miss Mustard Seed's Nancy stencil)

White paint (I used Annie Sloan Chalk Paint in Pure White)

Thick paper plate

Plastic spoon

Foam pouncers (larger one for stenciling and smaller one for making dots—mine are by Martha Stewart Crafts®)

Paper towels, folded

White furniture wax (I used Annie Sloan's white wax)

Wax brush

Before

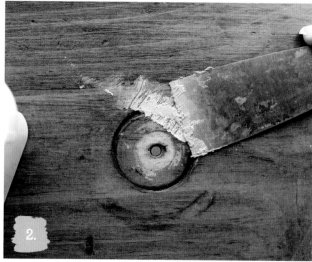

1. Clean and make repairs to your dresser as needed. Refer to page 182 for helpful tips on making repairs and prepping your piece for a makeover. This piece was in great shape for its age and didn't need any major repairs.

2. Remove the drawers. It seemed like the drawer pulls had been changed at some point, because there were deep grooves where the former pulls used to be. I filled those circles with wood filler and a scraper but otherwise left all the little nicks and dents alone as part of its character. Once dry, sand over the filled areas with 220-grit sandpaper.

3. Next, give your piece 2 to 3 coats of gray paint. I skipped painting the insides of the drawers because the wood was in good condition.

4. Always paint the inside of the frame where the drawers go. Once they're pushed in, you want the paint to peek through from underneath and on the sides, not the original wood. I do this for all of my makeovers to give them a more finished look.

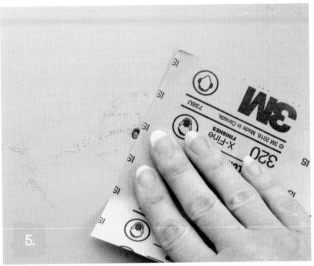

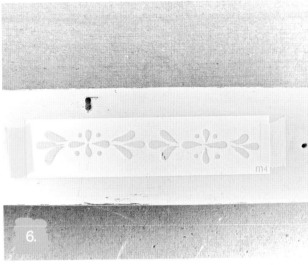

5. Lightly sand all over for smoothness with 320-grit sandpaper.

6. Tape your chosen stencil to the center of a drawer. Since this stencil is pretty simple, I started it off-center and then flipped it around later so there would be three flourishes centered on each drawer.

7. Get your white paint, strong paper plate, plastic spoon, large foam pouncer, and folded paper towels ready for stenciling. Scoop some paint onto the plate so it's easier to work with.

8. With the foam pouncer, dab it into the paint and then blot the excess off onto the folded paper towel. You don't want too much paint on the pouncer or you might end up with globs and drips under the stencil. Gently dab it onto the stencil, let it sit for 1 to 2 minutes to dry, and then go over it a second time.

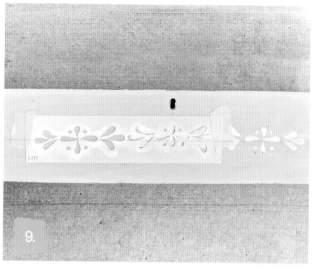

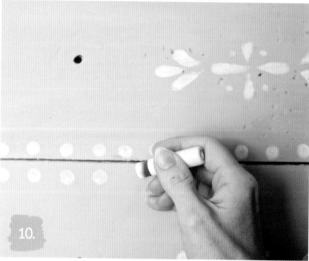

9. When that section was done, I flipped the stencil to overlap the center flourish and then repeated the previous steps, stenciling just the left area. Miss Mustard Seed's stencils are based on hand-painted designs, so they are not perfectly symmetrical. By flipping it over, the left and right flourishes end up being a mirror image of each other. If you're using a regular stencil, you shouldn't need to flip it.

10. After all the drawers are stenciled, add some whimsical dots along the edges with a small foam pouncer. Blot it on the paper towel first and then you can make several dots before dabbing it into the paint again. Don't worry about it being perfect.

11. For fun, add a stencil and dots to the sides of the dresser too!

12. Let the paint dry for about 10 minutes. Very lightly sand over the white painted areas with 320-grit sandpaper to give it a timeworn, faded look. Also sand near the edges of the drawers and dresser body to let the original wood show through some.

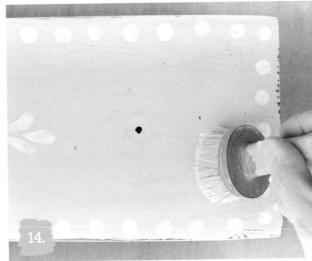

13. The wood pulls were still usable, so they were also painted gray.

14. Apply a topcoat to protect your beautiful work. I chose white wax to soften the gray tone a little more. Remember that wax takes about 30 days to fully cure, so be cautious setting things on top of the dresser for the first several weeks.

15. Be proud of your newest artistic creation!

Striped Chateau Dresser

French-themed makeovers have always been a weakness of mine, since I'm a complete Francophile and have been lucky to travel there twice. I thought this thrifted dresser would look perfectly Parisian with blue and white stripes and a sweet "Chateau" stencil on the front. In this makeover, you'll discover how to paint stripes without measuring and other tips for transforming a piece from blah to oh là là!

Supplies

Wood filler (I used Elmer's ProBond® wood filler)

Small scraper

220-grit sandpaper

Light blue paint (I used Annie Sloan Chalk Paint® in Duck Egg)

Paintbrushes

FrogTape® Delicate Surface painter's tape

White paint (I used Annie Sloan Chalk Paint in Pure White)

Small detail paintbrush

Chateau stencil (Fusion™ Stencil #17)

Foam pouncer

Black or dark gray paint (I used Annie Sloan Chalk Paint in Graphite)

Paper towel

320-grit sandpaper

Furniture wax (I used Annie Sloan's clear wax)

Wax brush

Lint-free cloth

New drawer pulls

Before

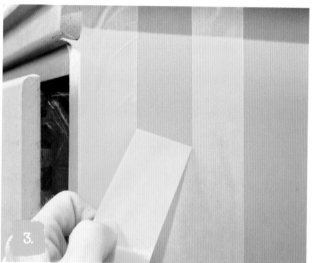

1. Although this dresser was plain, it had good bones. It's perfect for a creative makeover.

   Make any needed repairs and remove the old hardware. Fill in one hole on each side with wood filler and a scraper since we'll only need one hole for the new pulls. Let it dry and lightly sand with 220-grit sandpaper. Refer to page 182 for helpful tips on making repairs and prepping your piece for a makeover.

2. Paint the dresser with 2 to 3 coats of light blue paint and lightly sand until the surface is smooth. The very top will be painted white later.

3. Next you'll learn how to paint stripes without doing any tedious measuring. Decide how wide you want the stripes to be. I wanted these to be the width of two strips of tape. I also wanted the first stripe to overlap the corner because that's how my measurements worked out. Starting on one side, line up three strips of painter's tape. Then carefully remove the center strip.

4. Place that strip to the right of the third strip. Then remove the third strip you taped on, and place it to the right of the last strip.

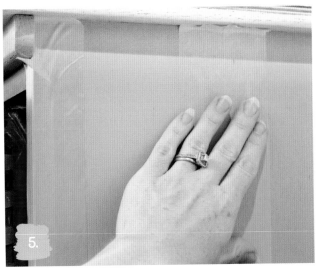

5. Press them flat into place. Now you have a non-taped area that's the width of two strips, and then a taped area of two strips.

6. Repeat the process until the left and right sides are both taped. On the front of the dresser, you will need to measure just to make sure that one stripe goes exactly down the center. Then work out from either side creating taped stripes. Press down over the tape to remove bubbles.

7. Paint over the blue areas with white paint. Again, work on one side at a time.

8. Once a side is painted white, wait a few minutes and while the paint is still slightly wet, carefully remove the tape to reveal straight stripes. If you do have any areas where paint got under the tape, use a small detail paintbrush to fix them. Finish each side and then paint the top of the dresser white too. Let the paint dry for about an hour before moving on to the next step.

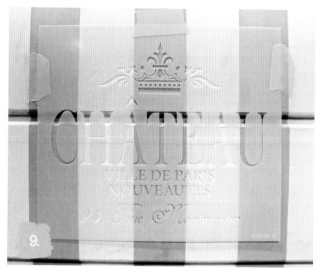

9. Center a stencil over the front of the dresser. Plan out where you want the words to go because you might have to reposition the stencil for each drawer. Use painter's tape to hold it in place.

10. Dab a foam pouncer into the black paint and blot it onto a paper towel to remove most of the paint. Less is more when you're stenciling.

11. Stencil the crown onto the top drawer.

12. It should dry within 1 to 2 minutes since you're only using a small amount of paint. Reposition the stencil and paint the next section onto the middle drawer.

13. Move the stencil to the bottom drawer to paint the bottom line.

14. Fill in the little gaps that the stencil left behind with a small detail brush. This makes it look less obvious that you used a stencil. Let everything dry for approximately 30 minutes.

15. Lightly sand the dresser with 320-grit sandpaper and wipe away the dust. Then apply clear wax as a topcoat, wiping away the excess wax with a lint-free cloth. Be careful with the dresser for about 30 days until the wax has time to fully cure.

16. Add new hardware that doesn't compete with your painted dresser, like these clear glass pulls. *C'est magnifique!*

Batik-Inspired MCM Nightstand

The clean, simple lines of mid-century modern furniture always draw me in. This thrifted nightstand is unique in that the wood was unfinished when I found it, and it almost looked handmade (although very sturdy and well-made). I wanted to do a bohemian, batik-inspired design on the drawers with small dots and chose an unconventional "paintbrush"—an eraser from a broken pencil.

Supplies

220-grit sandpaper

Primer (I used Zinsser B-I-N® Shellac-Based Primer)

Paintbrush for priming

Wood filler (I used Minwax® Stainable Wood Filler)

Small scraper

Yardstick

Pencil

Drill

3/16" (4.8-mm)-size drill bit

Safety glasses

Stain (I used Minwax® Wood Finish™ stain in Special Walnut)

Paintbrush for staining

Clean rag

Polyurethane (I used Rust-Oleum Varathane® water-based polyurethane in Crystal Clear Matte)

Paintbrush for applying polyurethane

White paint (I used Annie Sloan Chalk Paint® in Pure White)

Paintbrushes for painting

Painter's tape

Round shape for tracing (I used a lid from a snack container)

Blue paint (I used a Valspar paint sample called Indigo Cloth)

Pencil with an eraser

Paper towels

Furniture wax (I used Annie Sloan's clear wax)

Lint-free cloth

New drawer pulls

Before

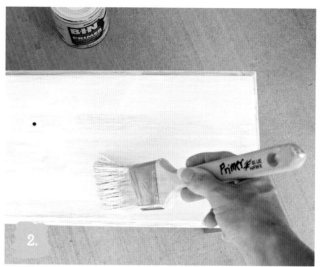

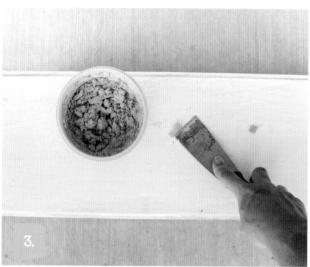

1. Clean and repair the nightstand as needed. This one didn't need any repairs, but I did sand it by hand to smooth out some rough areas. Refer to page 182 for helpful tips on making repairs and prepping your piece for a makeover.

2. Remove the drawers and give them two coats of primer to prevent the paint from soaking into the unfinished wood. Zinsser B-I-N® Shellac-Based Primer dries pretty quickly, so you don't have to wait more than 5 to 10 minutes before moving on. Lightly sand after each coat dries.

3. Around this time, I decided to switch the center pulls to two separate pulls for each drawer, so I filled the original holes with wood filler using a small scraper. After they dried, I sanded them smooth with 220-grit sandpaper. Usually you'll want to fill old holes and drill new ones before priming or painting—it's easier that way. In this case, I just needed to apply some primer again over the top of the dried wood filler.

4. To measure the new holes, hold a yardstick vertically to find the center of the drawer and mark it on both the left and right sides. Then turn the yardstick horizontally and line it up with the marks you just made. Decide how far from the edge you want the pulls and make another mark on each side. Repeat for every drawer.

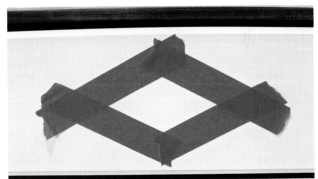

5. If you're not already, head outside (for easier cleanup) with your drawers and a drill. Remember to always wear the proper safety eyewear when using power tools! In my experience, most drawer pulls need a ³⁄₁₆-inch (4.8-mm)-size drill bit for drilling new holes. Drill two new holes where you marked on each drawer.

6. Stain the outside of the nightstand, brushing the stain on and then gently rubbing away the excess with a clean rag. Since this wood was unfinished, it took the stain really well and only needed one coat. Let it dry for at least 30 minutes, depending on the temperature and humidity. If in doubt, wait longer.

7. Protect the stained areas with at least two coats of polyurethane, letting each coat dry for about 20 to 30 minutes, depending on the temperature and humidity. The poly'd areas will be ready for light usage after about 24 hours.

8. Paint the drawers with 2 to 3 coats of white paint, sanding lightly between coats. Now it's time for the fun part—creating the batik design on the drawers. For this I used a yardstick, painter's tape, and even a round plastic lid from my toddler's snack container. My design inspiration was a batik rug I saw online.

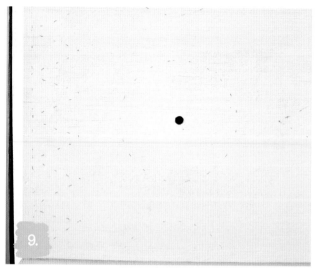

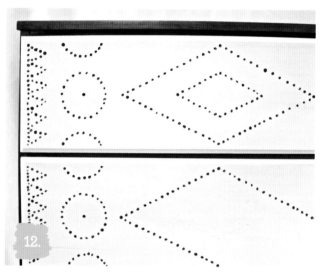

9. Use a pencil and draw little dots to outline your design. There's no wrong way to do it, just try to keep everything aligned and symmetrical.

10. Pull out the blue paint, a pencil with an eraser (I used half of a broken pencil that I found in my son's school supplies), and paper towels. Dip the eraser into the paint and then blot it on the paper towel once so it's not too wet. Then follow the lines that you drew on the drawers, making dots but not too close together, until the paint is used up. Then dip and blot it again.

You don't need to cover all the pencil marks you made—you can erase any leftover marks later. If you're right-handed, go from left to right so you don't smudge any of the wet paint while you're working.

11. I drew diamonds in the center of the drawers, circles around where the new pulls would go, and a triangle border down the left and right sides. Outline your design on all the drawers.

12. It's perfectly fine if the dots vary in size and some are darker than others—that makes it look more like an authentic batik pattern. Once you've finished, take a look and see if you need to add anything else to the design. Take a break and sleep on it if you need to! That's what I did, and I came back to it the next day with a clearer vision: more dots.

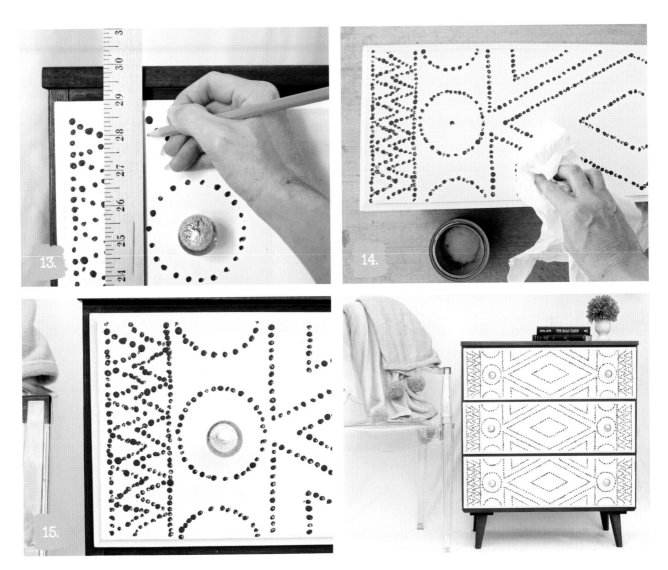

13. Use your tools again to mark where you want to add more. I even added smaller dots between the ones I had already painted to make the design fuller.

14. When you're happy with how it looks and the paint is dry, gently erase any leftover pencil marks. Don't sand the drawers after dotting—the raised texture is part of the charm.

Protect the drawers by rubbing a thin layer of clear wax over them with a lint-free cloth. The cure time for wax is about 30 days, so be careful not to bump or scratch the drawers.

15. Add some chic new hardware like these clear glass pulls, and your batik-inspired nightstand is ready for its grand debut!

Reupholstery
MADE EASY

You've been searching for months and finally found the perfect style of dining room chairs on Craigslist, but the fabric has worn thin on the seats. Would you still buy them? Or perhaps you've stashed away your grandmother's antique settee in storage, hoping to one day restore it to a beautiful, comfortable piece. If the thought of attempting reupholstery intimidates you, I'll show you that it doesn't have to.

There are a few things to know before you get started, though. First, you'll need to choose a durable fabric. In the following projects, I use duck cloth and even a painter's drop cloth. If the seat will get a lot of use, you might want to stay away from white or very light colors. Also, if you choose a striped or patterned fabric, you'll have to pay special attention when cutting and positioning it to keep the lines straight or the pattern direction consistent.

If your chair needs more than just new fabric, you may not know exactly what supplies you'll need until you start taking it apart. *Tip: It helps to take photos so you remember how to put it back together later!* First, unscrew the seat and set the screws aside to reuse. Then use an upholstery staple remover to take off the old fabric—you may want to keep it and label it to use as a pattern for the new fabric. For most chairs, if the cushion underneath the fabric needs replaced, that usually just requires new poly foam (1 to 2 inches [2.5 to 5 cm] thick) and cotton batting. Batting helps to hold the foam pad in place and makes for a smoother appearance under the new fabric.

Follow the steps in the subsequent makeovers to learn everything you need to know for basic (and a little more advanced) reupholstery: a simple chair makeover with reupholstered seat (page 49), a farmhouse-style sofa bench (page 53), and a French armchair featuring faux grain sack upholstery (page 61). Then hopefully you'll feel confident to tackle those dining chairs or your grandmother's settee. It really can be simple if you take it step by step!

← *Cotton Stem Sofa Bench (page 53), Armchair with French Grain Sack (page 61)*

Simple Chair Makeover with Reupholstered Seat

Basic chairs can be found in abundance at yard sales. I snagged this one for only ten dollars early one Saturday morning. Some people either don't have the creative vision or basic upholstery knowledge to transform an outdated chair into a unique piece for their living area or home office. I'd much rather update a thrifted chair for cheap in exactly my own style than pay a high price for a brand-new one. In this makeover, I'll walk you through how to change the upholstery on a simple chair so you can create your own custom piece!

Supplies

Screwdriver

Super glue and clamps, if needed (I used E6000)

Upholstery staple remover

Poly foam pad (I used a 1" [2.5-cm]-thick pad)

Sewing scissors

Cotton batting (I used Warm & White)

Heavy-duty stapler

Staples

Hammer, if needed

Durable fabric of choice

Neutral fabric for bottom side of seat (optional)

Beige paint (I used Annie Sloan Chalk Paint® in Country Grey)

Paintbrush

220-grit sandpaper

Furniture wax (I used Annie Sloan's clear wax)

Lint-free cloth

Before

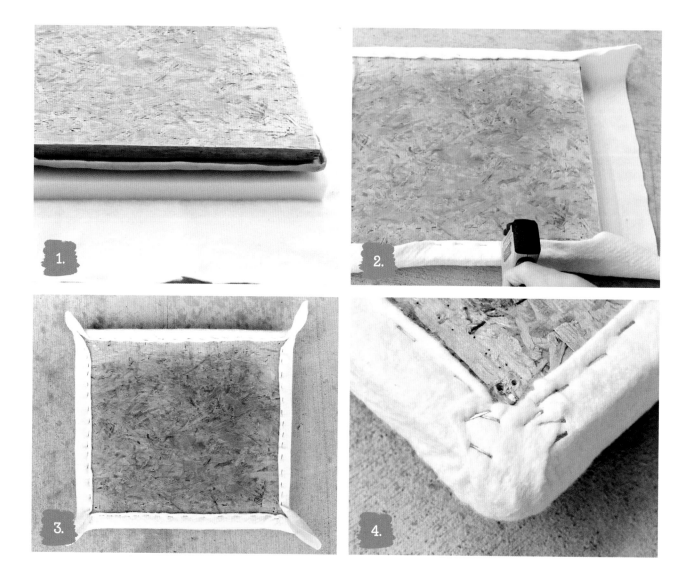

1. First, unscrew the seat from the frame and make any necessary repairs. Refer to page 182 for helpful tips on making repairs and prepping your piece for a makeover. I usually stay away from chairs that aren't completely sturdy, but this one had just a slight wobble, so I turned it over and put some clear E6000 glue on the joints. I left them clamped for about 24 hours to dry while I reupholstered the seat.

   Flip the seat over and remove the existing fabric and staples with an upholstery staple remover. You can use other tools instead, but your hands may end up blistered—ask me how I know! Examine the existing cushion to see if it needs to be replaced or just needs extra thickness. This cushion was in good shape but a little flat, so I added a 1-inch (2.5-cm)

   poly foam pad for a more comfortable seat. Cut the pad to the approximate size of the seat. Then cut the cotton batting 3 to 4 inches (7.5 to 10 cm) longer than each side of the seat.

2. Start with the front side of the seat by folding the batting over and stapling about an inch (2.5 cm) from the edge. You may want to slightly fold the edge of the batting before stapling for a straighter line. You may need to hammer the staples all the way in. Continue stapling the first side of the seat but stop about 1½ inches (4 cm) from the corners.

3. Turn the seat and staple the opposite side, pulling the batting taut. Continue likewise with the other two sides. You'll end up with the four corners sticking out.

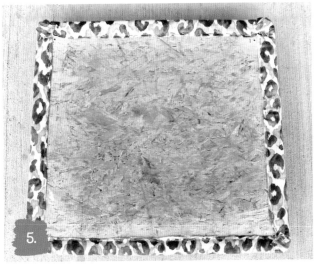

4. Corners can be tricky, so remember these tips: Don't let the batting get too thick when you're folding, and don't cover the holes where the screws go. I usually make one fold on each side of the corner, one side at a time. I cut the excess fabric underneath to keep the fold thin, pull tight, and add a few staples. Then I do the other side. It doesn't need to look perfect, but it needs to be secure. Continue with the other corners.

5. Make sure your chosen fabric is ironed—and if there's a pattern, that it's lined up how you want it. Cut the fabric like the batting, with an extra 3 to 4 inches (7.5 to 10 cm) all around the sides. Staple the fabric just the same as the batting—work on opposite sides, pulling taut, and save the corners for last.

6. If you want to hide the wood or your staples, you can cut a neutral shade of basic cotton fabric, fold the edges under, and staple it to cover the edges you've already stapled, but avoid covering the screw holes.

7. Now that the seat is done, paint the chair frame in a color that coordinates with the fabric. I gave this chair about three coats of paint, lightly sanded and distressed it with 220-grit sandpaper, and finally waxed it for protection. Since this is a simple piece without much area to cover, I applied the wax with a lint-free cloth instead of a brush. You can see in the photo how the wax deepens the hue of the paint, so keep that in mind.

8. Finally, screw the seat back onto the chair, sit yourself down, and relax in your latest makeover.

Cotton Stem Sofa Bench

I scored this small sofa bench for only ten dollars at a thrift store. The pink gingham fabric was definitely filthy, but the bench was otherwise in great condition. Upholstery projects like this aren't usually easy for a beginner, but if you take it step by step and have patience, anyone can learn how to do it. This bench now has a farmhouse vibe with new cotton stem fabric that will look beautiful in any urban or country cottage.

Supplies

Screwdriver

Upholstery staple remover

Needle-nose pliers

New fabric (I prefer duck cloth for upholstery)

Straight pins

Sewing scissors

Iron

Heavy-duty stapler

Staples

Hammer

Adhesive spray (optional)

New dust cover fabric (optional)

White paint (I used Annie Sloan Chalk Paint® in Pure White)

Paintbrush

Furniture wax (I used Annie Sloan's clear wax)

Wax brush

Lint-free cloth

Before

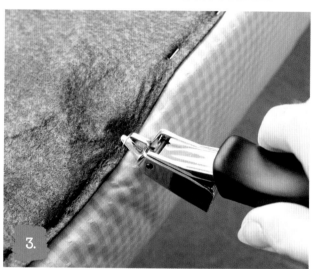

1. This sofa bench was structurally sound and didn't need repairs, but the dirty, dated fabric had to go! Refer to page 182 for helpful tips on making repairs and prepping your piece for a makeover.

2. Turn the bench over and unscrew the legs.

3. Use an upholstery staple remover to remove the staples from the dust cover. You can save it to reuse later if it's in good condition.

4. Any time you're doing a big upholstery project, I recommend taking a lot of photos when you're removing the old fabric so you can refer to them later when you're putting the new fabric on.

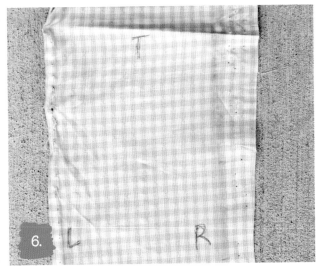

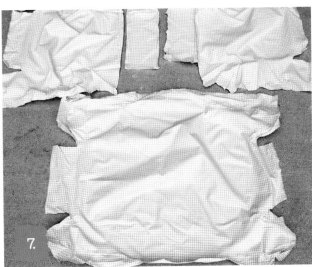

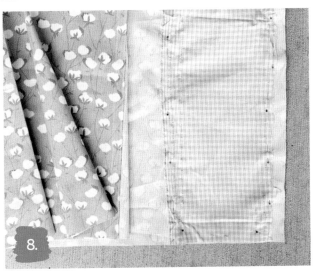

5. One section at a time, remove the staples and set the old fabric aside. Thankfully the foam and batting on this bench were in great condition and didn't need to be replaced.

6. If your new fabric has a pattern that has to face a specific direction, label the old pieces to save yourself time and frustration later. If you're new to reupholstering, you might want to skip this kind of pattern and choose a fabric without a directional design.

7. This small sofa bench had one large piece covering the middle and two pieces for each arm.

8. Use the old fabric as a pattern for cutting the new fabric. Make sure the outside (the "good" side) is facing the same direction for both pieces, and that your labels are facing the correct way. Use straight pins to hold the pieces together and then cut. I always cut larger than the original piece, because it's better to have extra just in case you need it than to run out of room later. If the old fabric has little notches or slits, cut them into the new fabric also. Iron the new pieces.

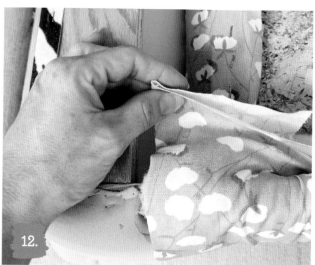

9. I started with the middle piece, tucking the ends down between the seat and the arms.

10. When upholstering a seat like this, always start with two opposite sections. Then turn the piece and do the other two opposite sections, saving the corners for last. Here I stapled the back side first, slightly folding and tucking the fabric on curves. Then I turned the bench and pulled the fabric tight while stapling the front side.

11. Next, staple the two ends near the arms. Remember that the staples will be hidden, so they don't have to look perfect—they just need to be secure. Gently hammer any staples that don't go all the way in.

12. Now fold and tuck the corners in and staple them. You're done with the middle section!

13. Lay out the fabric over one arm. Make sure it's facing the same direction as the seat fabric.

14. Tuck one side in between the arm and the seat.

15. Turn the bench and staple the part you just tucked underneath the bench. Don't pull the fabric too much because you'll need some extra later.

16. Tuck and fold the bottom corners in place.

17. Now it's time to tackle the rounded arm. Hopefully you took photos when you removed the old fabric earlier. Start on one side, making small folds in the excess fabric and stapling each one underneath the arm. You'll end up with about five folds and then turn and do the other side of this arm.

18. When both sides of the arm are finished, the loose fabric between them should be stapled right across the bottom under the curve.

19. Turn the bench over to attach the last piece of fabric. Make sure the pattern is facing the correct direction. Leave the left and right ends hanging over on each side for now. Fold the wide end over a little and staple it right across the last row of staples you made.

20. Fold the left and right ends inward like so, spray some adhesive in there if you'd like, fold the entire section up and over the bottom edge of the bench, and then staple it into place.

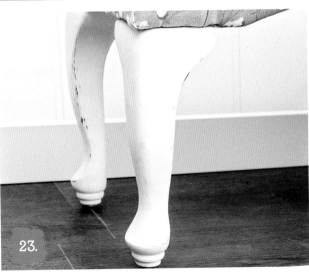

21. The end of the bench looks professional, and that little fabric piece hides so many imperfections.

22. Add a dust cover underneath (also to hide the not-so-pretty parts). I used a neutral-colored fabric that I already had instead of the original black dust cover.

23. Paint the sofa legs white, protect them with clear wax using a lint-free cloth, and screw them back into place.

Armchair with French Grain Sack

Did you know that you can buy a canvas drop cloth from the home improvement store, wash and dry it, and then it will look and feel just like a vintage grain sack? Add some stenciling and you will end up with a very antique-looking French grain sack, which looks gorgeous on a chair needing a fresh look. This armchair and its twin were only twenty dollars at a yard sale. I didn't need them at the time, but I'd have been crazy to pass them up. (Maybe I was crazy for buying them!) The fabric on the seats was worn thin, which could intimidate anyone not familiar with upholstery. In this project, we'll go in-depth so you can learn how to reupholster a chair like this one and discover tips for making it more unique and personal to your taste.

Supplies

Screwdriver

Upholstery staple remover

Small flathead screwdriver

Needle-nose pliers

Off-white paint (I used Annie Sloan Chalk Paint® in Old White)

Paintbrush

320-grit sandpaper

Furniture wax (I used Annie Sloan's clear wax)

Lint-free cloth

Sewing scissors

Cotton batting (I used Warm & White)

Canvas drop cloth—washed, dried, and ironed

Heavy duty stapler

Staples

Hammer

Air compressor and staple gun

Hot glue gun and glue sticks

Jute cord

Jean Marquet Feed Sack with Stripe stencil by Euro Stencil Designs on Etsy

FrogTape® Delicate Surface painter's tape

Foam pouncer

Taupe paint (I used Annie Sloan Chalk Paint in Coco)

Paper towels

French Bee Stencil by StudioR12 on Etsy (I only used the crown)

Black or dark gray paint (I used Annie Sloan Chalk Paint in Graphite)

Toffee gimp trim

Before

1. This lovely French-style armchair had great bones, but the fabric was in desperate need of replacement. Remember to refer to page 182 for helpful tips on making repairs and prepping your piece for a makeover. Yuck—not lovely at all! New grain sack–inspired fabric will be a huge improvement on this armchair.

2. I was lucky with this chair because the seat was held on with screws. If your seat doesn't unscrew, search for "reupholstered chair makeover" on my website, Girl in the Garage®, to learn from my other tutorials. Unscrew the seat and start removing

the trim and the fabric with a staple remover. Be careful not to rip the fabric. Just set it aside for now.

3. Next, take the back of the seat apart. Take photos of how everything looks to help you remember later when putting it back together.

4. The chair back had a little groove all the way around where 12,826 staples were hiding. Do your best to remove as many of them as possible without damaging the wood that will be visible. Use a small flathead screwdriver and needle-nose pliers to help. Don't overwork your hands or

5.

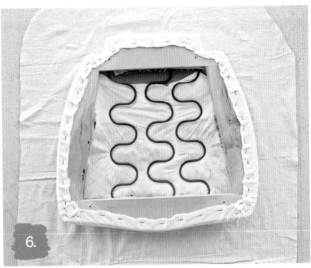

6.

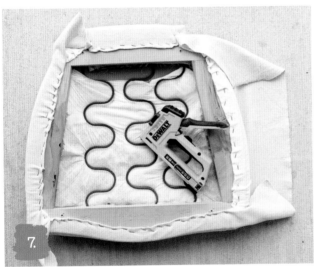

7.

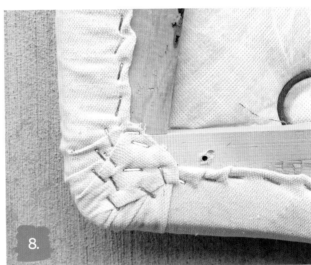

8.

arms. Take it slow and spread this step out over a few days if needed.

5. Paint, lightly distress, and then wax the chair frame—similar to Step 7 of the Simple Chair Makeover with Reupholstered Seat on page 51.

6. Use the old seat fabric as a pattern to cut the cotton batting and the drop cloth, making them a little larger than the original pieces. The foam for the chair didn't need to be replaced, but

I did add new batting to the seat for extra softness. Staple opposite sides first, and then do the corners last. Gently hammer any staples that don't go all the way in.

7. Then staple the drop cloth over the batting, folding the edges under first. This helps prevent fraying, which drop cloths tend to do.

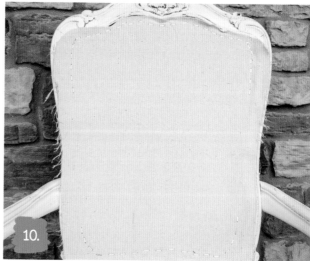

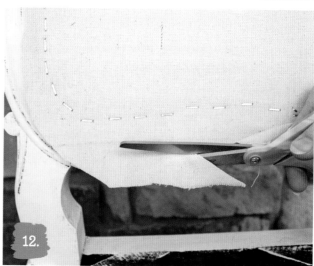

9. For the back of an upholstered seat, I always use an air compressor and a staple gun. It's a little more work to set up, but once you get the hang of it, it's really easy to use, and it will save you so much time and energy. I used to be scared of tools like this, but now I don't know how I ever did this kind of upholstery without it! Center the fabric that will be seen from the back side of the chair and put a few staples into the top on the front side of the chair. Then pull firmly and put a few staples into the bottom.

10. Alternate working on the top and bottom, keeping the staples consistent and always pulling the fabric firmly.

11. Take turns stapling on either side until you meet in the middle on the left and right. Go back and add more staples if you have any gaps.

12. Cut away the excess fabric, but still leave about 1 inch (2.5 cm) all the way around.

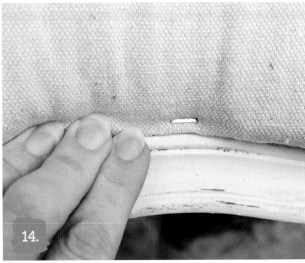

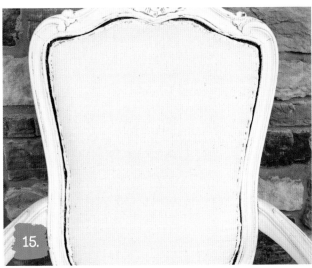

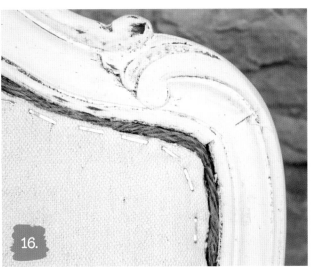

have any gaps.

12. Cut away the excess fabric, but still leave about 1 inch (2.5 cm) all the way around.

13. Place the back foam into place. Start at the top again, tucking the back layer of fabric inward, then tucking the excess fabric for the front layer behind the foam, and then stapling. Put a

few staples across the top.

14. Repeat for the bottom, tucking the fabric edges inward and then stapling around the foam. Try to keep the staples close to the chair frame.

15. Just as before, take turns stapling the top and bottom and

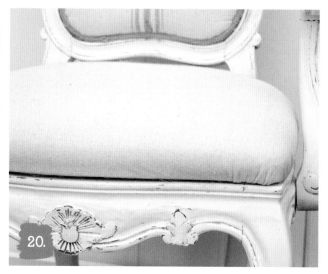

17. Center the feed sack stripe stencil and tape it in place. Dab a foam pouncer into taupe paint and then blot it onto a paper towel to remove most of the paint. Then rub the pouncer gently over the stencil to create the appearance of grain sack stripes. If your stencil isn't long enough, reposition it lower and finish the stripes. Let it dry for a few minutes.

18. Next, stencil a crown at the top with black paint, and then the French words below it. Remove the stencil and let the paint dry for a few minutes.

19. Hot glue the gimp trim around the chair back to hide the staples. Start somewhere on the bottom so the trim ends aren't so obvious. Slightly overlap the ends. You can also choose to add gimp trim around the bottom of the seat. If the seat is attached to the chair frame, I would 100 percent always add the trim. In this case though, it's up to you since there will still be a small gap between the seat and the frame. You can also add upholstery tacks over the trim if you'd like.

20. Screw the seat back onto the chair. Admire your hard work at turning an ugly yard sale find into a gorgeous French armchair with antique grain sack upholstery.

How to Create Depth
WITH LAYERS AND TEXTURE

Painting a piece of furniture with two or more layered colors creates depth and texture that's reminiscent of a work of art. Mastering this technique can take your makeovers to a whole other level. Think about famous artists like van Gogh or Monet—don't their paintings often look vivid and three-dimensional?

It does take practice to make the technique look natural and not overdone—so pull out a surface to paint on and use the projects in this chapter to get started. You'll up your furniture refinishing game in no time!

In this chapter, you'll learn how easy it is to do the dry brush technique on a French provincial nightstand (page 71), how to create a vintage French finish with layered paint colors (page 77), and finally, how to do raised stenciling with spackling on a nightstand (page 81).

Creating a Vintage French Finish with Layers (page 77), Embossed Nightstand (page 81)

Dry Brushed French Provincial Nightstand

I was so excited to find this dixie house nightstand for ten dollars at a yard sale that I didn't even notice the broken foot! Thankfully it was an easy fix, and I'll show you how I did it. The original yellow was dated and had to go, but I wanted to keep the sophisticated style, so I dry brushed it with similar colors and a hint of metallic. With dry brushing you can add subtle contrast, texture, or even a weathered look to your piece. It's simple to do and makes a big difference—I use this technique on a lot of my makeovers.

Supplies

Random orbit sander

Safety glasses and face mask for protection

Wood filler (I used Elmer's ProBond® wood filler)

Small scraper

220-grit sandpaper

Beige paint (I used Annie Sloan Chalk Paint® in Country Grey)

Paintbrushes

Off-white colored paint (I used Annie Sloan Chalk Paint in Old White)

Small detail paintbrush

Paper towels

Metallic paint (I used Modern Masters shimmer/satin sheen metallic paint in Champagne)

320-grit sandpaper

Furniture wax (I used Annie Sloan's clear wax)

Lint-free cloth

Before

1. This nightstand had a lot of chipping that had to be addressed first.

2. Remove the drawer and sand down the chipped areas with an electric sander. If your piece isn't real wood like mine, don't sand too heavily. Try to smooth it out as best you can.

3. Next, repair any areas that need it. The foot on this table was missing a chunk, but thankfully it was still stable anyway. Refer to page 182 for helpful tips on making repairs and prepping your piece for a makeover.

4. To repair the foot, first turn the table over. Using a wood scraper, fill the area with wood filler while trying to mimic the shape of the opposite foot.

5. Let it dry, then sand it smooth with 220-grit sandpaper while shaping it. Your dry time will vary depending on how wide and deep the area is that you're filling.

6. Apply another layer of wood filler if needed, repeating steps 4 and 5 until the foot looks whole again.

7. Here is the finished leg. Once it's painted, you'd never know there was a chunk missing before!

8. Paint the table beige with 2 to 3 coats for complete coverage. Let the paint dry for at least 20 to 30 minutes between coats.

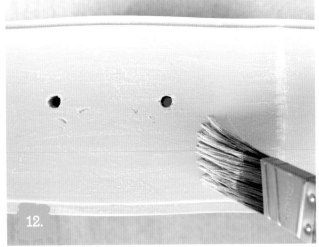

9. Use a small brush to carefully paint all the little grooves off-white.

10. Prepare to dry brush the table. Get another brush and fold some paper towels in half.

11. Dip the tips of the paintbrush bristles into the off-white paint, and then dab the brush onto the paper towel. Get all the excess paint off so that the brush is basically "dry."

12. Then lightly brush across the entire table so that the paint leaves a soft layer of color and adds texture. Don't add too much—but if you accidentally do, you can always brush on more of the original color to tone it down.

13. Next, add a layer of metallic paint using the same dry brushing technique for a subtle shine.

14. My table had too much variation in color, so I ending up lightly brushing on more of the original beige paint. The dry-brushed colors still peek through and look so pretty, especially when shimmering in the light.

15. Gently sand any bumpy areas with 320-grit sandpaper. Remember that dry brushing creates texture, so don't worry about getting it really smooth. Finally, protect your piece by rubbing on clear wax with a lint-free cloth. Wait about 30 days for regular usage so the wax has time to fully cure.

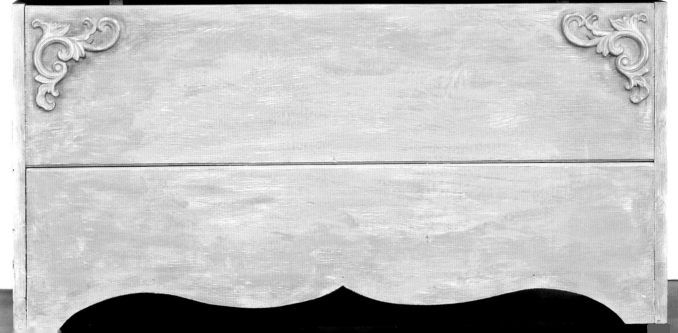

Creating a Vintage French Finish with Layers

Any plain piece can become one of a kind with appliques, and no one would guess they weren't there originally. Then take your makeover one step further by creating a vintage French finish with layered paint colors and distressing. It's easy to learn, and you'll have your friends saying oh là là in no time!

Supplies

Decorative appliques (preferably wood)

Super glue (I used E6000)

Zinsser B-I-N® Shellac-Based Primer

Paintbrush for priming

Light gray paint (I used Annie Sloan Chalk Paint® in Paris Grey)

Paintbrushes for painting

Darker gray paint (I used Annie Sloan Chalk Paint in French Linen)

220-grit sandpaper

White paint (I used Annie Sloan Chalk Paint in Pure White)

Paper towels

Black or dark gray paint (I used Annie Sloan Chalk Paint in Graphite)

Small detail paintbrush

Furniture wax (I used Annie Sloan's clear wax)

Lint-free cloth

Before

1. Clean your piece and make any needed repairs. Refer to page 182 for helpful tips on making repairs and prepping your piece for a makeover. This chest was old but in good condition—no repairs needed.

2. Choose appliques to give your piece more character. I used three and only one was made of wood, but the wood applique was by far the easiest to glue onto the chest.

3. Glue them on one at a time with a super glue like E6000. Hold them in place until they feel secure. The complete drying time can take up to 24 hours, so give it time to cure.

4. I glued the wood applique to the top back and the others to each corner of the front.

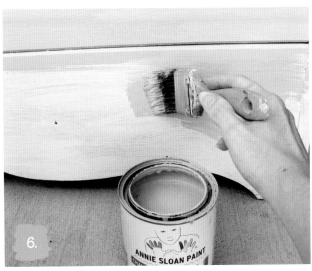

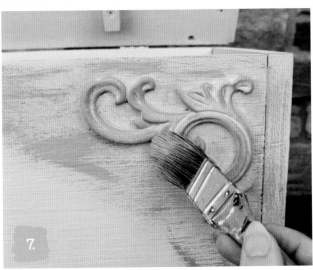

5. Because the chest was stained so dark, I primed it before painting to avoid bleed-through. You may need 2 to 3 coats of primer to fully cover a dark piece of furniture. Let it dry for 20 to 30 minutes between coats.

6. Next, give your piece 2 to 3 coats of light gray paint for full coverage, letting it dry again for about 20 to 30 minutes between coats.

7. Then lightly brush on some darker gray paint around the edges and over the appliques.

8. Sand what you've already painted and let some of the white primer peek through.

9. Next, dip the tips of your bristles into white paint and blot it onto a paper towel so most of the paint comes off. Then, dry brush the white over the appliques and lightly over the rest of the chest.

10. Sand the chest again so the paint colors are more blended and it's less obvious where one stops and another starts.

11. Finally, very lightly dry brush some dark gray or black paint over the appliques.

12. Protect your work by applying clear wax with a lint-free cloth, letting the wax cure for 30 days before regular usage.

Congrats—you've achieved a vintage French finish by layering paint colors, dry brushing, and distressing. The appliques turn any plain piece of furniture into a uniquely custom showpiece!

Embossed Nightstand

This vintage nightstand was well-made (by Pennsylvania House) but was definitely outdated. It was just the right style for a new embossed—aka "raised stenciling"—makeover. This technique adds unexpected texture with just a stencil and spackling. It's also meant to look imperfect, so there's really no way to mess it up! Add some fun layered colors for a truly unique and creative makeover.

Supplies

Moorish Fleur De Lis stencil from Royal Design Studio Stencils

Stencil spray adhesive (I used the Tulip® brand)

Spackling (I used DAP DryDex® Spackling with dry time indicator)

Putty knife/scraper

320-grit sandpaper

Turquoise paint (I used Annie Sloan Chalk Paint® in Provence)

Paintbrushes

Gold paint (I used DecoArt Americana Décor® metallic paint in Gold)

White paint (I used Annie Sloan Chalk Paint in Pure White)

Furniture wax (I used Annie Sloan's clear wax)

Lint-free cloth

New drawer pulls

Before

1. This was a sturdy piece with an outdated style that mostly just needed cleaning. Refer to page 182 for helpful tips on making repairs and prepping your piece for a makeover.

2. Choose a good-quality stencil (not a thin flimsy one) and spray the back with adhesive.

3. Lay it over the nightstand and press it down. Normally when painting a stencil, I start in the middle. But this project is meant to be a little more casual/imperfect, so I started in the upper corner.

4. Apply the spackling over the stencil with a putty knife. DAP DryDex® Spackling is cool because it starts off kind of purple-pink and then dries to white when it's okay to sand or paint. Just like when painting a stencil, less is more. You only need a thin layer of spackling. If you put a little too much on though, you can sand it down later.

5. Once the stencil is covered, wait a minute and then carefully lift it away. Don't let the stencil dry with spackling all over it. Wait a few more minutes until the spackling isn't so wet and then reposition the stencil to keep the pattern going. Continue for the entire front of the nightstand.

6. Let the table dry overnight to make sure the spackling is completely dry. Then lightly sand it with 320-grit sandpaper to even out bumps and flatten thicker areas. If you have any smudges, you can also sand or scrape those away. Remember: imperfect is okay!

7. Paint the nightstand turquoise and let it dry for 20 to 30 minutes. This is just a base coat, so the coverage doesn't need to be flawless.

8. Next, lightly brush gold paint randomly over the turquoise. This will provide a soft shimmer under the next layer.

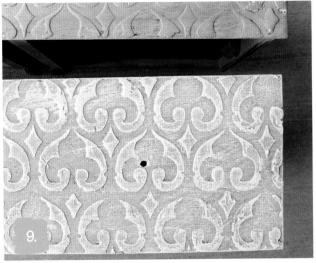

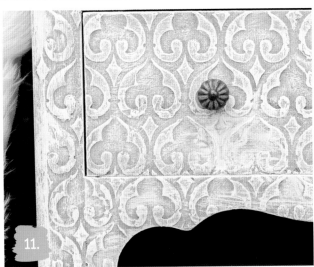

9. Finally, paint the nightstand white. but only lightly dry brush over the embossed areas. Learn more about dry brushing in the Dry Brushed French Provincial Nightstand makeover on page 71.

10. Gently sand again and then apply clear wax with a lint-free cloth for protection. Wait 30 days for the wax to cure before putting the nightstand to use.

11. Add new pulls for the final finishing touch. This little embossed nightstand is definitely one of a kind!

How to Transfer
IMAGES ONTO FURNITURE

Adding image transfers to furniture is another creative technique that isn't too difficult once you've learned it. There are really easy methods, such as rub-on transfers, and more time-consuming ones, such as using an overhead projector or transfer paper. You can master any of these with the right products and a little practice.

With an overhead projector, you can paint an image as big as you want. I got my projector from a school that no longer needed it. You can look for a used one at schools, libraries, or in online ads. If you do a lot of makeovers, it's an awesome tool to have around. You will also need transparency paper and a heat-safe surface when using an overhead projector.

For smaller furniture, you can transfer an image with carbon transfer paper, as long as you don't need it to be larger than the paper itself. Find the paper at craft stores or online.

Within the last few years, rub-on transfers have become very popular because there are so many designs available and you literally just rub them onto the surface with a stick. There are all different sizes and colors available. I recommend trying rub-on transfers from Iron Orchid Designs or Re-Design with Prima.

In this chapter, you'll see examples of these techniques on three different makeovers. First, see how a vintage bench is updated with a distressed paint finish and a rub-on transfer (page 89). Next, a small table makeover gets a medallion image with transfer paper and a Sharpie (page 93). Finally, an antique armoire gets a complete overhaul, including a vintage bicycle advertisement on the doors (page 99). Add any graphics or words you can imagine to furniture with one of these image transfer techniques.

Medallion Side Table (page 93), Bicycle Armoire (page 99)

Bienvenue Bench

There's something so welcoming about having a bench near the entrance to your home. It invites friends to sit and chat, kids to rest for a few minutes after a long day at school, and it can add a certain charm to your décor. This bench looked like it belonged in a farmhouse, so I updated it with neutral distressed paint and a simple, yet striking, image transfer. Read on to learn how easily you can update your furniture with a rub-on transfer like this one.

Supplies

Beige paint (I used Annie Sloan Chalk Paint® in Country Grey)

Paintbrush

220-grit sandpaper

Clean rag

Tape measure

Rub-on transfer and rubbing stick (I used an Iron Orchid Designs transfer)

Painter's tape

Furniture wax (I used Annie Sloan's clear wax)

Wax brush

Lint-free cloth

Before

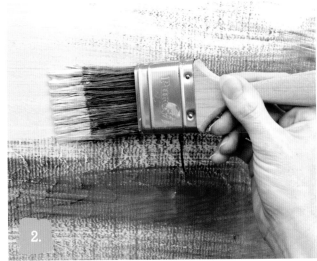

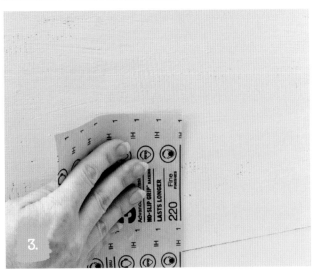

1. Clean and make any necessary repairs. Refer to page 182 for helpful tips on making repairs and prepping your piece for a makeover. I only needed to lightly sand it to smooth a few rough areas.

2. Start by painting the bench. Give it a couple coats, but don't worry about full coverage. You want the wood to peek through in some areas. Let it dry for a few hours.

3. Sand the bench to smooth the finish and give it a naturally distressed look. Focus on the curves and edges first, then move on to random smaller areas on the rest of the bench. Remember that you want it to look natural and somewhat weathered. If you sand off too much, you can always go back and add more paint to that area. Wipe off the dust with a clean rag.

4. Measure the center of the bench where you want the graphic to be. Remove the plastic backing of the rub-on transfer and then tape the graphic into place with painter's tape. Rub over the image repeatedly with the rubbing stick in every direction.

5. Slowly lift the edge of the graphic sheet. If the image hasn't fully transferred, lay it down again and continue rubbing. It may take 15 to 20 minutes, or longer for larger graphics.

6. Once the image has transferred, apply a topcoat over the entire bench for protection. I used Annie Sloan's clear wax and a wax brush. When waxing, work in small sections and then wipe away the excess with a lint-free cloth. The cure time for wax is about 30 days, so be gentle with your piece for the first month or so. Finally, welcome friends and family to stop by for a visit and chat on your newly refinished bench!

Medallion Side Table

Give a damaged antique table new life with some TLC and a unique medallion graphic. Discover the simple way to do an image transfer without any fancy equipment or expensive supplies; all you need is special transfer paper. This trashy ten-dollar table can now be used and treasured for years to come.

Supplies

Random orbit sander

Safety glasses and face mask for protection

Super glue (I used E6000)

Gray paint (I used Annie Sloan Chalk Paint® in Paris Grey)

Paintbrush

Painter's tape

Medallion graphic

Paper cutter

Clear tape

Tape measure

Carbon transfer paper

Pencil

Black Sharpie

320-grit sandpaper

Furniture wax (I used Annie Sloan's clear wax and black wax)

Lint-free cloths

Before

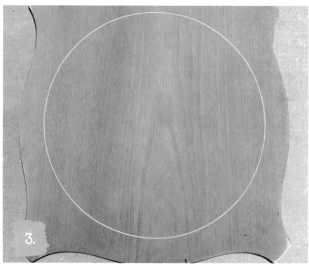

1. First, clean and repair your piece as needed. Refer to page 182 for helpful tips on making repairs and prepping your piece for a makeover.

2. The top of this antique side table was badly damaged, so I used an electric sander to smooth it out. Remember to always wear safety glasses and a mask when using power tools.

3. The wood grain and the inlaid circle on top were beautiful after sanding.

4. The legs were a little wobbly, so I flipped the table over and applied E6000 to each joint and let it sit for about 24 hours.

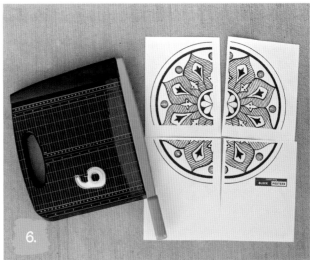

5. Next the table was painted a light gray, except for the top. Use painter's tape if needed to keep the paint from going past the edge.

6. Find a medallion design online and save it to your computer. Tip: Find lots of free graphics on The Graphics Fairy website at thegraphicsfairy.com. I wanted a larger image than what could fit onto a regular sheet of paper, so I went to the Block Posters website at blockposters.com, uploaded the medallion graphic and enlarged it to be able to fit within the circle on the table. It printed onto four sheets of paper, which I cut with my paper cutter and then taped together. Print your image onto regular computer paper, not cardstock.

7. I slightly overlapped 1½ sheets of carbon transfer paper face down on the center of the table. The visible sides of the inlaid circle and a tape measure helped me center the medallion graphic over the transfer paper, and I taped everything in place with painter's tape.

8. Trace over the graphic with a pencil, pressing firmly. Don't use a pencil that's very sharp. A thicker, duller tip works better. You may decide to leave out certain elements of the design, and that's perfectly fine. Make it your own style! I opted for a little bit simpler look than what was printed originally.

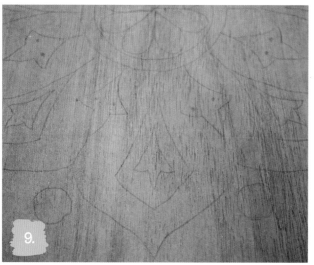

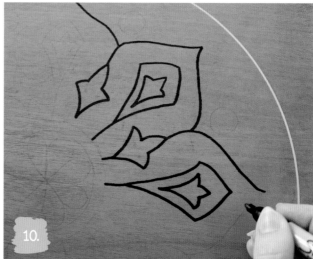

9. Here you can see the faint lines that were transferred when I traced the graphic.

10. Now trace over those lines with a Sharpie (or a thin paintbrush and paint, if you have a steady hand). Go slowly and have patience. It's exciting to see your image transfer come to life! When the design is finished, let the ink dry for at least 24 hours.

11. Lightly sand over the painted areas to accentuate the lines and curves. This table is meant to look aged yet elegant.

12. Apply clear wax with a lint-free cloth as a topcoat.

13. Immediately follow it with black wax. If you apply too much black wax, you can wipe some away with a little more clear wax.

14. The black wax helps highlight all those details and makes it look less freshly painted. Let the wax cure for about 30 days before beginning to use the piece regularly.

15. Your one-of-a-kind side table with a medallion image transfer deserves to be proudly displayed. And no one has to know how easy it was to do by yourself!

BICYCLE

THE MOST COMPREHENSIVE CYCLING CATALOGUE FREE.

POPE MFG CO., 79 FRANKLIN ST., BOSTON.

Bicycle Armoire

Antique armoires were built to last, so it seemed this one was worthy of saving even though it needed a lot of work. In this tutorial, learn how to strip away old paint, add new shelves inside, and paint a vintage advertisement graphic using an overhead projector. This is truly a one-of-a-kind piece that will make a statement in any bedroom. If you don't have an overhead projector, you can try this project with transfer paper like in the Medallion Side Table project (page 93).

Supplies

Paint stripper (I used Citristrip®)

Paintbrush for stripper (not one of your nicest ones)

Safety accessories: gloves, goggles, face mask (read the stripper label and follow the safety precautions)

Scraper

Random orbit sander

Primer (I used Zinsser B-I-N® Shellac-Based Primer)

Paintbrush for priming

White paint (I used Annie Sloan Chalk Paint® in Pure White)

Paintbrushes for painting

320-grit sandpaper

Graphic printed onto transparency paper

Overhead projector

Heat-safe surface

Pencil

Thin black Sharpie

Yardstick

Black paint (I used Fusion™ Mineral Paint in Coal Black)

Small detail paintbrush

Table saw (or have wood cut at the hardware store)

Safety glasses and hearing protection

1" (2.5-cm) wood panels

Small screws

Screwdriver

Wood glue

Level

Nails

Hammer

Furniture wax (I used Annie Sloan's clear wax)

Wax brush

Lint-free cloth

Magnetic closure

Small hooks

Keyhole covers

New knobs or pulls

Before

1. Clean and make a plan for any repairs and updates to the armoire. Remember to refer to page 182 for helpful tips on making repairs and prepping your piece for a makeover.

   The inside of this piece wasn't in great shape, so it was going to get some changes and be painted also.

2. First the old yellow paint had to be removed. Follow the directions on your paint stripper bottle. Guy in the Garage brushed it on and almost immediately it started bubbling up and eating away at the old paint.

3. For the most part, it was easy to scrape off. Just be careful around corners and grooves so you don't gouge the wood.

4. I was planning to paint the armoire anyway, so the wood didn't need to be in perfect condition. We did have to sand it all over to make sure the finish was really smooth. I also removed the hanger hardware on the left inside the armoire so we could add more shelf space.

5. With the wood stripped and sanded, it definitely needed several coats of primer (outside and inside so it wouldn't bleed through later). Then it was painted in several coats of white paint and finally sanded for a smooth finish.

6. Next is the fun part—adding the image transfer! Choose your graphic (I found this free downloadable graphic online from The Graphics Fairy website) and then print it with a regular printer onto transparency paper to be used on an overhead projector.

7. Set up the projector on a heat-safe surface and make sure the image is centered on the front of the armoire. Get comfy because this next part can take a while depending on how complex your graphic is. But try to get it all traced in one sitting, because if the projector gets bumped or moved, it will be very difficult to get everything lined up exactly the same way again.

8. Trace the image onto your piece with a pencil. Go slowly, and if you make a mistake, just erase it and keep going. For the bicycle spokes, I skipped tracing them for now because I knew there'd be no way I could get the lines straight later.

9. Once the image is transferred, go over the lines with a thin-tip Sharpie. You can use a small paintbrush instead if you have a very steady hand, but I don't! You may need a multi-pack of Sharpies if your image is large. I ended up filling in the thicker areas later with a paintbrush.

10. Use a yardstick to draw the spokes on straight. You can draw with a pencil first or just skip directly to using a Sharpie.

11. Fill in the tires and bigger words with a small paintbrush and black paint.

12. After the paint dries, go back and gently erase any visible pencil marks.

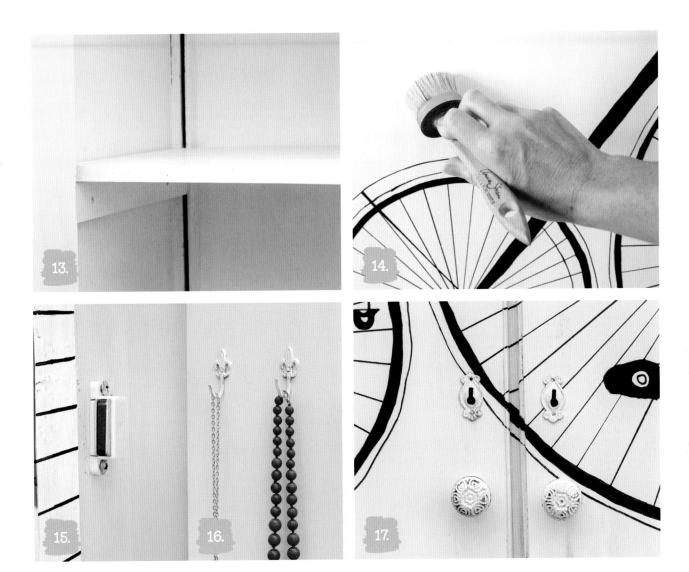

13. Cut two new shelves 1 inch (2.5 cm) thick to fit in the left side of the armoire. Also cut one brace for each shelf (just for the left side, so you won't be screwing all the way through the exterior of the armoire). Paint the shelves and braces white. Install the brace on the left with small screws and wood glue where you want the shelf to go. Put some wood glue on top of the brace and then lay the shelf on top, using a level to make sure it's straight. Screw it in straight down into the brace and then directly through the center wall from the right side (you probably want a helper for this).

14. Brush on clear wax to protect the piece inside and outside, wiping away the excess with a lint-free cloth. Remember that wax takes about 30 days to fully cure, so be patient before starting to use this piece regularly.

15. I added a new magnetic closure on one side.

16. I also added some small hooks (painted white) inside the door for hanging jewelry, scarves, or other little treasures.

17. Finally, new knobs and painted keyhole covers finish off the look for this armoire transformation. It makes a nostalgic statement with the vintage bicycle ad on the outside, yet it is also functional with shelves and hanging space inside.

The Ancient Art
OF DECOUPAGE

For hundreds of years, people have been gluing paper cutouts on surfaces as decoration—first on tomb walls, then lanterns, boxes, and other small objects. In modern times, artists can use decoupage to personalize almost any type of home décor or furniture. I've done this on tables, armoires, dressers, bookcases, drawers, storage boxes—even an old garage hardware organizer.

Once you've chosen your item to decoupage, next choose what you'll decoupage onto it. Scrapbook paper, wrapping paper, wallpaper, posters, book pages, tissue paper, napkins, greeting cards, magazine clippings, fabric, etc. are all good choices. Consider the size of your piece when choosing which type of paper or fabric to use. There are several types of decoupage glues, but I prefer matte Mod Podge® and a foam brush for application.

Although you can decoupage onto many different surface types, we'll be focusing on wood furniture here.

How to Decoupage onto Furniture

1. Lightly sand the surface to make it more smooth. Glossy surfaces may need a little extra sanding to help the paint and glue adhere. Refer to How to Know When to Prime on page 182 to help determine if you need to prime after sanding.

2. Next, paint your surface. Choose a color that's close to the background (or other dominant color) of the paper you've selected.

(continued)

← *Old World Cabinet (page 113), Repurposed Hutch to Dollhouse (page 119)*

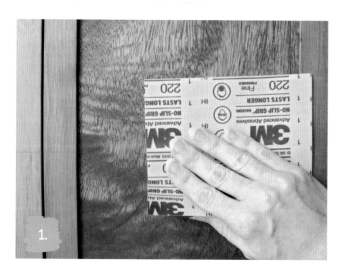

3. Measure and cut your paper to the correct dimensions. Use a paper cutter for short edges or a yardstick and scissors for long edges. If you're working inside a drawer, you may want to leave a little excess around the edges and then trim it with an X-Acto knife after gluing. And keep in mind that a lot of old drawers have sides that are not equal lengths, so measure every side individually!

Tip: Your paper doesn't have to have straight lines. You might decide to cut out flowers or other unique shapes for your project.

4. Apply a light but full-coverage coat of matte Mod Podge onto the surface with a foam brush. If you have a small area, cover it entirely. For a larger area, work in sections because Mod Podge tends to dry quickly. Avoid globs of glue and missed areas.

5. Press the paper down over the glued area, starting with one edge. Very gently rub and push out any bubbles. Keep rubbing and smoothing for several minutes as this section starts to dry. Wipe away excess glue around the edges with a napkin. Repeat for the rest of the paper.

6. Let the project dry completely (it will feel dry to the touch within a couple hours). Protect your work with a topcoat of Mod Podge. Apply in thin, even layers. You can sand between coats if desired, but I rarely do. Some surfaces like tabletops will need several coats for lasting durability. Wait 4 weeks cure time for regular usage. You can choose to use Mod Podge Hard Coat as a topcoat if you're working on an area that may get a lot of wear and tear, like a tabletop.

In this chapter, there are three different decoupage makeovers to inspire you. First, a plain vintage dresser gets a mod update with Aztec-print wrapping paper on the drawers (page 109). Then an antique cabinet is given a masculine makeover with a vintage-inspired world map inside (page 113). Finally, a lonely hutch that lost its desk becomes a charming dollhouse with colorful patterned walls and floors (page 119). You can customize any of these ideas for your own creative decoupage projects!

Aztec Dresser with Wrapping Paper

Here's a plain-front dresser with so many possibilities. I found this one at a nonprofit thrift store that funds a local men's shelter. I always prefer to buy pieces at those types of stores before browsing personal sales ads.

The mid-century modern style of this guy seemed like it was destined for this Aztec-print wrapping paper I've had stashed away. Gift wrap is for more than just gifts, right? In this tutorial, you'll learn how to update any flat-front dresser with decoupage and wrapping paper.

Supplies

Random orbit sander

Safety glasses and face mask for protection

White paint (I used Annie Sloan Chalk Paint® in Pure White)

Paintbrush

Furniture wax (I used Annie Sloan's clear wax)

Wax brush

Lint-free cloth

Wood filler (I used Elmer's ProBond® wood filler)

Small scraper

220-grit sandpaper

Yardstick

Pencil

Drill

³⁄₁₆" (4.8-mm) size drill bit

Wrapping paper

Scissors

Decoupage glue (I used matte Mod Podge®)

Foam brush

Paper towels

New knobs or pulls (I used unfinished wood pulls painted white)

Before

1. This big beast was heavy and had a lot of scratches, so first it was sanded with an electric sander. Refer to page 182 for helpful tips on making repairs and prepping your piece for a makeover.

2. Remove the old drawer pulls and paint everything with 2 to 3 coats of white paint (or whatever color looks good with your chosen paper). Let it dry for at least an hour and then protect the body with clear wax, wiping away the excess with a lint-free cloth. The cure time for the wax is about 30 days, so be gentle with the piece while waiting for it to cure.

3. If you decide to change the hardware, you might need to fill the old holes with wood filler using a scraper. Once dry, sand over them with 220-grit sandpaper. And if you're like me and had already painted the drawers, add more white paint over the wood-filled areas.

4. Measure where you want new pulls to go, mark with a pencil, and drill new holes. For tips on how to measure for the placement of new hardware, see the Batik-Inspired MCM Nightstand project on page 41.

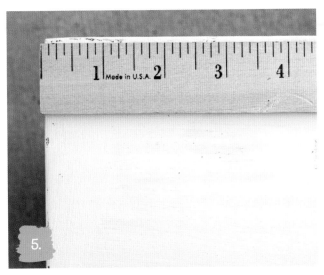

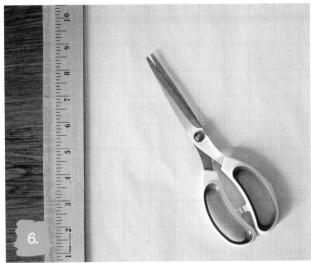

5. Measure the drawers to see what sizes you need to cut the paper. Don't assume all the drawers are the same size.

6. Lay out the wrapping paper on a clean, flat surface. Use a yardstick and pencil to mark the drawer sizes. Cut the paper for each drawer.

7. Stand the drawers on their backs. Set the paper on each drawer to check the size. Trim the paper if needed.

8. With your paper lined up on the drawer, set something heavy on one end to hold it in place. Then lift the other end of the paper and wipe Mod Podge® onto the drawer with a foam brush in thin, even coats. Work in small sections at a time before the Mod Podge starts to dry. I did about four sections per drawer since they're quite long. Keep paper towels nearby to wipe up any excess glue.

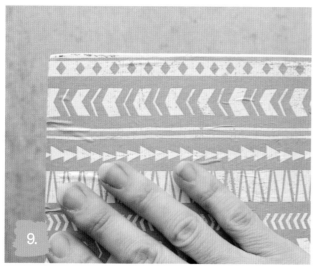

9. Press the paper down carefully over the glue. Lightly press and rub over the area to get rid of air bubbles and wrinkles. Don't press too hard or you could rip the paper.

10. Now that one end is glued, you don't need anything heavy on the other end. Finish gluing the paper down one section at a time, working slowly and carefully. Repeat for all the drawers.

11. When all the drawers are dry, brush a final coat of matte Mod Podge on top of the paper for an added layer of protection.

12. Finally, add new pulls. I painted unfinished wood pulls white to not distract from the bold Aztec drawers.

Old World Cabinet

Give an antique cabinet old world charm with decoupage and a vintage map. Learn how to decoupage a poster onto the back of a cabinet, paint some parts for contrast, and revive the unpainted wood parts to showcase its natural beauty. This custom style is sure to add vintage character to your home.

Supplies

Wood glue

Long clamp

Long, thin flathead screwdriver

Paint, similar color to the poster background (I used Annie Sloan Chalk Paint® in Old Ochre)

Paintbrushes

Large map poster (This one is from zazzle.com)

Yardstick and pencil

Scissors

Decoupage glue (I used matte Mod Podge®)

Foam brush

Paper towel

L-shaped shelf brackets

Small screws

Power driver/drill

Hammer

Paint for the outside of the cabinet (I used Annie Sloan Chalk Paint in Graphite)

320-grit sandpaper

Furniture wax (I used Annie Sloan's black wax)

Lint-free cloths

Hemp oil (I used natural hemp oil from The Real Milk Paint Co.®)

New knobs or pulls

Before

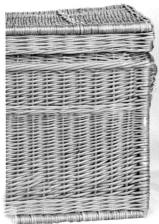

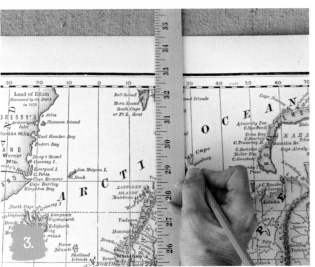

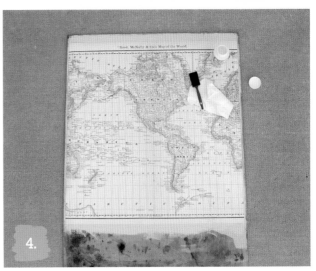

1. Clean and repair the cabinet if needed. Refer to page 182 for helpful tips on making repairs and prepping your piece for a makeover.

2. The top became separated from the rest of this cabinet on one side, so we added wood glue and left it clamped for about 24 hours to fully dry. As you can see, I got excited and started painting before this repair was made. Usually you should make any fixes before painting!

Carefully remove the back panel. I used a long, thin flathead screwdriver wedged like a lever between the back and the rest of the cabinet. Slowly push the back away, trying not to damage anything. As the nails start to become loose, remove them and keep them together in a safe place to reuse later. Work carefully until the entire back panel can be separated.

3. Paint the front of the back panel a similar color to the background of the poster you've chosen. I ordered a large poster from zazzle.com, but I knew that there would still be about 1 inch (2.5 cm) exposed above and below of just the painted panel. Lay the poster out and measure it with a yardstick. Make sure it's centered where you want it, marking the sides to be cut. Trim away the excess pieces.

4. Place the poster over the board exactly where you'd like. Gather your Mod Podge®, foam brush, and paper towel (in case of glue drips) to decoupage the poster on.

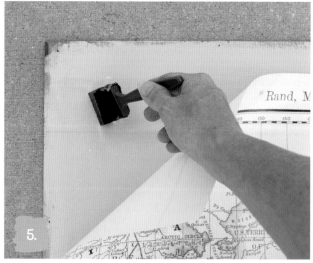

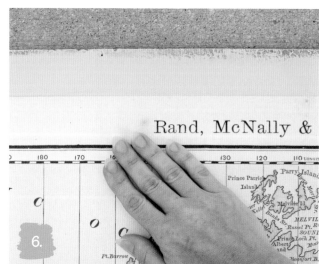

5. Start at one top corner and work in sections, applying a thin, consistent layer of Mod Podge directly onto the board with a sponge brush and then carefully laying down the poster.

6. After each section, press down continuously across that area for several minutes to smooth out any air bubbles. I just use my hands—no fancy tools required! Typically, I work my way across the top first, then down both sides at about the same time, and finally across the bottom. This helps minimize any large air pockets that could happen if you don't work in that order. Since this poster was going across the back of a cabinet and will be protected inside, I didn't feel the need to put a topcoat of Mod Podge over it. Set aside the panel to dry while you work on the rest of the cabinet.

7. Inside the cabinet, all the old shelf brackets were either rusted or missing. I replaced them with new bronze L-shaped brackets with screw holes underneath. Screws are usually optional, but they were necessary here (installed with a power driver/drill) because the shelves weren't quite perfectly rectangular and would've been wobbly otherwise. Then reattach the back panel with the existing nails and hammer.

8. Next, give the outside of the cabinet two coats of paint, letting it dry for 20 to 30 minutes between coats. Leave some of the original wood exposed—the inside, the top, front legs, and some of the detailed areas. This adds contrast so those special details stand out. Go over the painted areas with sandpaper to lightly distress and age the piece, focusing on the edges, curves, and lines so the original wood can peek through.

9. Apply black furniture wax with a lint-free cloth over the painted areas for protection. Work in small sections, rubbing the wax into the piece and then wiping away the excess with another cloth. The piece will be ready to stand up to regular use after the wax has cured for about 30 days.

10. Finally, use a lint-free cloth to rub hemp oil over the unpainted wood areas to revive their finish.

11. Dress up the cabinet with beautiful new pulls that complete your vision for the makeover.

Repurposed Hutch to Dollhouse

As a young girl, I loved spending hours pretending in an imaginary world with my dollhouse. So, when I found this lonely vintage hutch, I thought what better way to rescue it than to repurpose it into a sweet home for a tiny family? Just add walls and doorways, and then let your own imagination run wild while decorating each room and adding extra details. Make each day brighter for your dolls with colorful patterns on the walls and floors. This fun decoupage project is sure to bring a smile to any child's face.

Supplies

1" (2.5-cm)-thick pine wood

Table saw (or have wood cut at the hardware store)

Safety glasses and hearing protection

Drill

Screws

Primer (I used Zinsser B-I-N® Shellac-Based Primer)

Paintbrush for priming

White paint (I used Annie Sloan Chalk Paint® in Pure White)

Paintbrush

320-grit sandpaper

Furniture wax (I used Annie Sloan's clear wax)

Lint-free cloth

Dolls and dollhouse furniture (for estimating the appropriate height of the walls and doors)

Pencil

Scrapbook paper in a variety of colors and fun patterns

Paper cutter

Decoupage glue (I used matte Mod Podge®)

Foam brush

Paper towels

Hammer

Thin 1½" (4-cm) nails

White cardstock

Scissors

Safety kit for securing the dollhouse to the wall if small children will be playing with it

Before

1. This hutch was in great condition, and the shelves were the perfect height for a dollhouse. The only thing it was missing was a bottom board. I cut sturdy pine to the size of the base and secured it with a drill and screws. Refer to page 182 for helpful tips on making repairs and prepping your piece for a makeover.

2. Prime the piece first, and then paint it white. Don't worry so much about getting even coverage on the areas that will be covered in paper. Lightly sand with 320-grit sandpaper for smoothness.

3. Protect the painted areas by applying clear wax with a lint-free cloth. Don't wax the areas that you're planning to decoupage. Also, remember that wax has a cure time of about 30 days, so be more careful using it during that time.

4. Measure inside the shelves to determine how tall and deep the dollhouse walls should be. Plan for the doorways to be taller than your doll family. Stagger the walls so they're not directly in a vertical line. You may want to stagger where the doorways go just for fun. Cut pine for the interior walls.

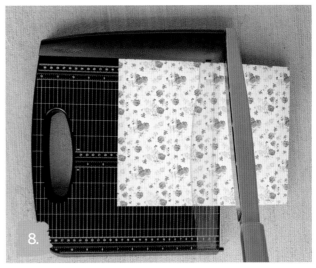

5. Set up furniture in the house to figure out exactly where you want the walls to be.

6. Trace around the walls with a pencil and set them aside. Paint the wall edges that will be facing outward and inside the doorways too.

7. Decide which paper to use on the walls and floors in each room.

8. Cut the paper as needed using a paper cutter for straight lines. You may need to cut little notches out of wall pieces depending on the hutch's design, or cut smaller pieces to reach a doorway that you traced.

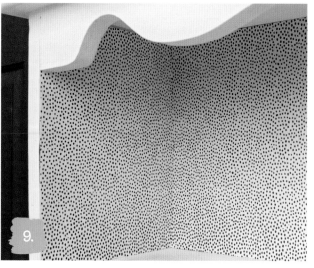

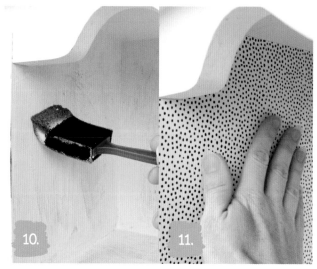

9. Double check that the paper fits before gluing it on.

10. Use a foam brush to apply an even, thin coat of Modge Podge® onto an exterior wall of one of the rooms, taking care to reach the edges.

11. Carefully lay the paper in place and smooth out any bubbles or wrinkles. Continue until that room is finished, and then complete the other walls in the dollhouse. (Glue the floor paper in place for the bottom floor only—not the other floors yet!)

12. Lay the internal walls facedown and trace them onto the paper for that room. Cut them out and decoupage the paper onto the walls.

13. Starting with the bottom floor first, slide the internal wall into place. Note: This photo does show the middle floor.

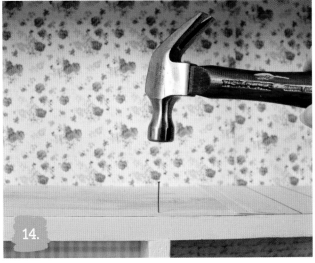

14. Tip the dollhouse over and hammer a couple nails in through the bottom. Then set the house upright again and hammer a few nails downward into the top of that wall. Now you can glue the floor paper into place for the second story (glue it over the top of the nails you just hammered). Install the next wall just as you installed the first, then glue the floor paper for the top floor and hammer that wall into place.

15. Where two different pieces of flooring or walls come together, cut a small strip of cardstock and glue it on with Mod Podge.

16. To add an extra special touch, decoupage the outside of the dollhouse with brick-printed paper. Also add a thin coat of Mod Podge over the top of all of the glued papers for extra durability.

17. Set up the furniture and have your doll family move into their new home. Let your imagination run wild with decorating it like a real house! This piece can also double as a whimsical bookcase if your child is either too young for playing with dolls or has outgrown them.

Creating a High-End Look with
UPHOLSTERY TACKS AND NAILHEAD TRIM

There's just something about the added touch of upholstery tacks to complete a beautiful reupholstered bench or a one-of-a-kind furniture design that screams high-end. But that "champagne taste" doesn't have to come with the hefty price tag. You can easily do it yourself with supplies from your local craft store and instantly transform a piece from meh to marvelous. Upholstery tacks and nailhead trim look beautiful on chairs, benches, dressers, tables, headboards, mirrors . . . use them anywhere you want to ramp up the wow factor.

Each project may differ in the way you decide to apply the tacks, but the overall steps are very similar. *Tip: If this is your first time using this method, you might want to practice on a smaller piece before jumping into a huge project.* Here are some tips to guide you through this makeover technique:

First, complete your project. Decorative upholstery tacks are like the sprinkles on the icing of your cake and should be added as one of the final steps of your makeover. Tacks come in many different finishes and textures, so choose one that complements your piece and then buy more than you think you'll need, just in case.

For a big piece like a dresser, draw out your design on paper first, and then draw little dots on the drawers with a pencil as a guideline. *Tip: Avoid hard woods like oak, because it will be extremely difficult to hammer in the tacks.* For an upholstery project, your tacks will follow a natural line near a straight edge or curve depending on the piece.

(continued)

Reupholstered Bench with Upholstery Tacks (page 129), Glamorous Nailhead Dresser (page 135)

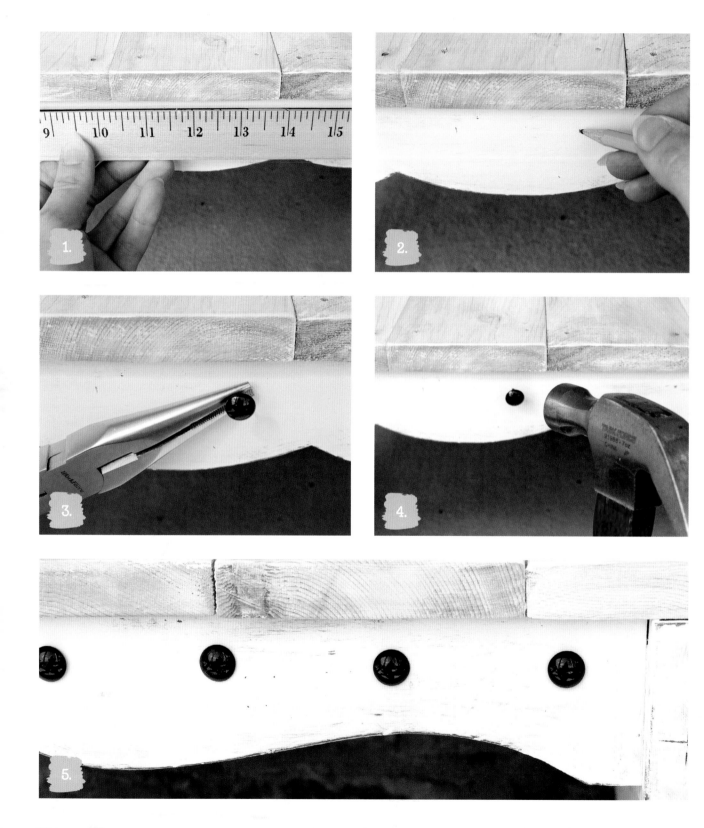

How to Add Upholstery Tacks to Furniture

1. If you're adding the tacks in a straight line, measure the length of your piece and determine how far apart you want the tacks to be. Then mark either the center point or an equal distance from the center. For example, the length on this piece is 24 inches (61 cm), and 12 inches (30.5 cm) is the midpoint. I decided to add a tack every 2 inches (5 cm) on the odd numbers, so 11 inches (28 cm) and 13 inches (33 cm) will be my middle tacks since they're both an equal distance from 12 inches (30.5 cm).

2. Mark a dot with a pencil everywhere you want a tack to go. You may decide to space your tacks 1 inch (2.5 cm) apart. Do whatever looks good to you. Just remember that if you're hammering lots of tacks instead of using nailhead trim, it will take more time and energy, and there will also be more room for error.

3. Gently tap the tack into place with a hammer or rubber mallet. Once it's standing on its own, you may want to hold it steady with needle-nose pliers so you don't smash your fingers.

4. Try to hammer straight and firmly to prevent the tack from bending or breaking. If you do have a mistake, remove the bent tack with the pliers and try again with a new tack. You may have to make a small repair to the wood afterward.

5. Continue until your upholstery tacks are all in place and your project looks fabulous.

In the following pages, you'll be inspired by two makeovers that use upholstery tacks and nailhead trim. First, a reupholstered bench is updated with new fabric, custom trim, and tacks (page 129). Then a plain dresser is given the star treatment with nailhead trim and tacks hammered into the front of the drawers for a sophisticated, modern look (page 135).

Reupholstered Bench with Upholstery Tacks

Benches are some of my favorite pieces to update, and if they have upholstery, that makes them even better. There's nothing like ripping off that old dingy fabric and making the seat more comfortable and stylish. Finally, finish it off with custom trim and upholstery tacks for a more glamorous look. Your friends will be jealous of your high-end makeover at a fraction of the cost!

Supplies

Screwdriver

Upholstery staple remover

2" (5-cm)-thick poly foam cushion

Scissors or electric knife

Cotton batting (I used Warm & White)

Durable fabric of choice

Heavy duty stapler

1" (2.5-cm)-wide trim (I used dark natural cotton webbing)

Sewing machine

Thread the same color as the trim

Hot glue gun and glue sticks

Upholstery tacks (I used Woodpile Fun!™ decorative upholstery tacks in antique brass)

Hammer

Needle-nose pliers

Yardstick

Paint (I used Annie Sloan Chalk Paint® in Old White)

Paintbrush

220-grit sandpaper

Furniture wax (I used Annie Sloan's clear wax and dark brown wax)

Lint-free cloths

Before

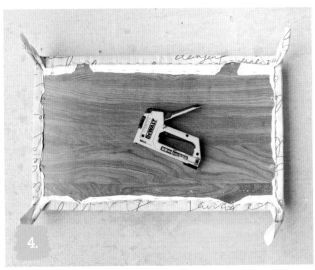

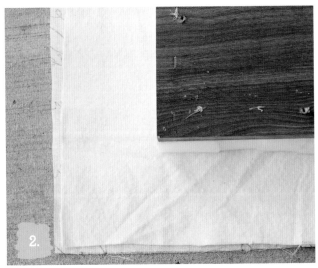

1. First, unscrew the seat from the frame and make any needed repairs. Refer to page 182 for helpful tips on making repairs and prepping your piece for a makeover. Thankfully this bench was quite sturdy, so I skipped to reupholstering the cushion.

   Lay the seat upside down and remove the old fabric and staples with an upholstery staple remover. Refer to Reupholstery Made Easy on page 47 for more specific upholstery advice. The following is an overview.

2. Since the old cushion was thin, I replaced it with a new 2-inch (5-cm) poly foam cushion cut to size. Also cut batting and fabric 3 to 4 inches (7.6 to 10 cm) wider than the seat all the way around.

3. Next, staple new cotton batting over the cushion. Start with one side, then the opposite, and then the two ends. Leave space around the screw holes and fold the corners in tight.

4. Staple the new fabric over the batting just as described in the previous step. Fold the edges under for a more finished look.

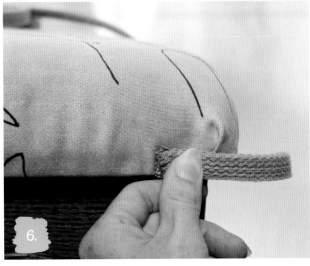

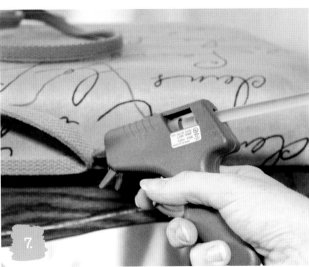

5. Next, select your trim for this project. I found the perfect color and texture webbing to use, but at 1 inch (2.5 cm), it was too wide. My solution was to fold it in half lengthwise and sew it so that it would be only half an inch (1 cm) wide. Make sure to run several rows of stitches across both ends to help prevent fraying. Leave a little extra length on the trim just in case. You'd rather have too much than not enough.

6. Now it's time to hot glue the trim into place, all the way around the bottom of the fabric. You can place your seat back onto the frame for this step to get a feel for what it will look like, but don't screw it back on yet. Start your trim in an inconspicuous area like the back or side, and not directly on a corner.

7. Work in sections, applying about 6 to 8 inches (15 to 20 cm) of hot glue directly onto the trim and then pressing it firmly onto the seat fabric in a straight line. When you reach the beginning of the trim where you started, cut the end if needed, apply a thin line of hot glue down the edge to help prevent unraveling, and then push the trim down so they meet.

8. Upholstery tacks will add that extra bit of special bling to this project. Start on one side of the bench and hammer a tack near each corner.

9. You can use needle-nose pliers to hold the tack in place and protect your fingers from getting smashed. Then find the middle of the bench with a yardstick, and hammer a tack there. After that I worked on half the trim at a time. I put a tack directly in between the one by the corner and the one in the middle. Then I put one directly in the middle of those two. You can eyeball it, but it helps to double check spacing with a yardstick.

10. Keep going until all your tacks are in place and evenly spaced out on each side. It worked out so that I had a tack directly over where the two ends of the trim met up, so it hid any imperfections there. In total I used about 75 tacks for this project.

11. Next, paint the frame of the bench and then sand it lightly for smoothness and a slight distressed look.

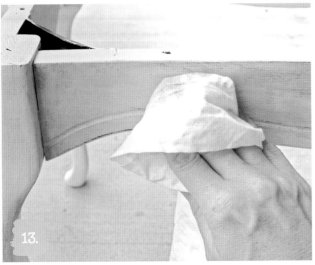

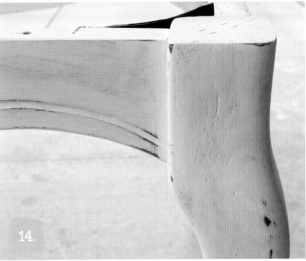

12. Apply a topcoat for protection—in this case a combination of clear and dark furniture wax, which also gives a naturally aged look and tones down the brightness of the paint. Using a lint-free cloth, wipe the clear wax thinly onto an entire side first, and then wipe a layer of dark wax over it with a different cloth. If it gets too dark, wipe over that area again with a little more clear wax, and that will remove some of the dark. Wax takes about 30 days to fully cure.

13. Repeat for each side until you're happy with how aged or "dirty" it looks.

14. For reference, here's a view of how the bottom corner of the seat should look when you're finished.

15. Finally, screw the seat back onto the frame.

16. Stand back and admire your reupholstered bench makeover, complete with new trim and fancy tacks. What other ideas do you have for using upholstery tacks in your projects?

Glamorous Nailhead Dresser

Nailhead furniture looks so high-end but usually costs a small fortune. I love using tacks to create beautiful, interesting designs on furniture (I even had one of those pieces featured in *Better Homes and Gardens* magazine in 2016). Learn how to create a glamorous look yourself with upholstery tacks and nailhead trim for a fraction of what expensive designer furniture costs.

Tip: This technique works better on softer woods, not hard woods like oak. If you're not sure of the wood type, try a test piece in an inconspicuous area first and see if the tack goes in easily.

Supplies

Random orbit sander

Safety glasses and face mask for protection

Wood filler (I used Elmer's ProBond® wood filler)

Before

Scraper

220-grit sandpaper

Gray paint (I used Annie Sloan Chalk Paint® in French Linen)

Paintbrush

Furniture wax (I used Annie Sloan's clear wax)

Lint-free cloth

Paper

Pencil

Yardstick

Needle-nose pliers

Upholstery tacks (I used Dritz Home® Decorative Nails in smooth nickel)

Hammer or rubber mallet

Flathead screwdriver

Toothpick (I used an upholstery needle because it was nearby)

320-grit sandpaper

Dritz Home® Decorative Nailhead Trim in silver/smooth nickel

Tin snips

New drawer pulls

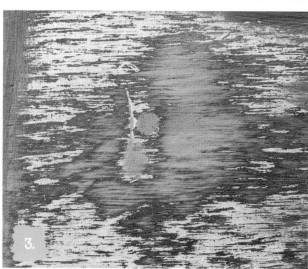

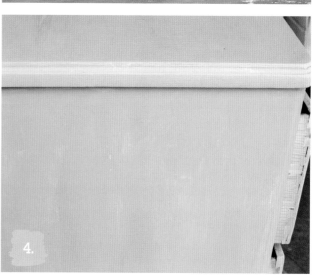

1. This dresser was already half sanded, but there was still a lot of texture from the previous paint. Refer to page 182 for helpful tips on making repairs and prepping your piece for a makeover.

2. Sand the surfaces smooth with a random orbit sander.

3. Using a scraper, fill one of the old hardware holes on each drawer side with wood filler, let it dry for at least 30 minutes, and then sand smooth with 220-grit sandpaper.

4. Paint the dresser with 2 to 3 coats of gray paint, letting it dry for about 20 to 30 minutes between coats. Then apply a topcoat like clear wax with a lint-free cloth. Remember that wax takes about 30 days to cure, so be gentle with your piece for the first several weeks.

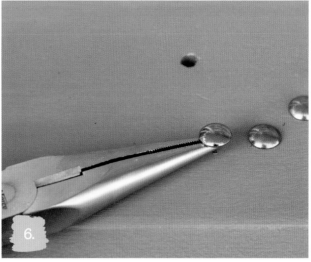

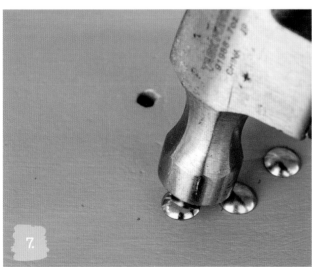

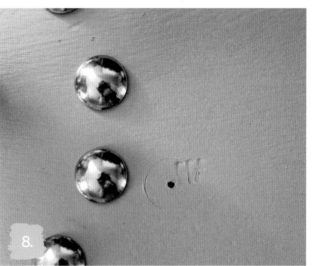

5. Draw out a plan for the tack design on paper. I changed my mind several times before (and even during) this project, and having a sketched image definitely helps. Following your drawing, use a yardstick to keep your design elements evenly spaced out and then draw light dots on the drawer with a pencil. Do one drawer at a time in case you need to make any changes.

6. Use needle-nose pliers to hold the tacks in place.

7. Gently use a hammer or rubber mallet to tap the tacks completely in.

8. It's common that you might nail a tack in the wrong spot, one might get bent and need to be pulled out, or the top might break off and the bottom need to be removed. If the top is still there, use a small flathead screwdriver as a lever to lift the tack out. You can also use the needle-nose pliers if needed. Once the tack is out, you may have a little dent in the wood from whatever tool you used.

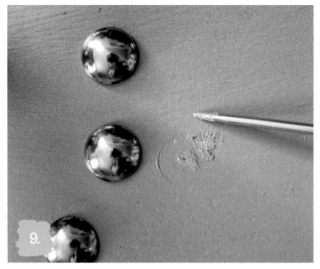

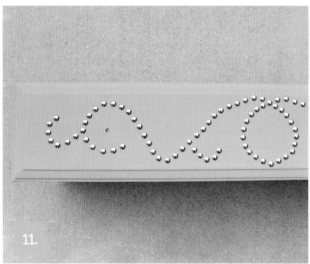

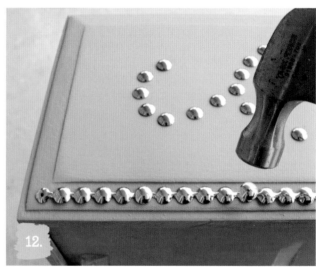

9. Get a tiny amount of wood filler on a toothpick or needle and rub it over the nail hole and dent.

10. After it dries, use the very corner of 320-grit sandpaper to smooth the area. Then paint and wax over it like before.

11. Finish hammering all the tacks into the drawers.

12. Now take the nailhead trim and start to add it across the length of the drawer near the bottom. This trim is really easy because you only hammer a tack into pre-spaced holes, which are spaced about 5 heads apart. When you start, skip the very first hole and then the very last hole, which are directly on the corners of this drawer. (Of course, your drawer might be different, so lay the trim out first to see where to start and end it.) Cut the trim with tin snips.

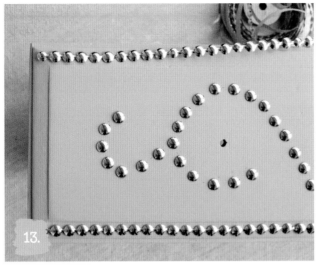

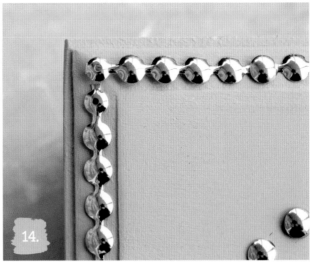

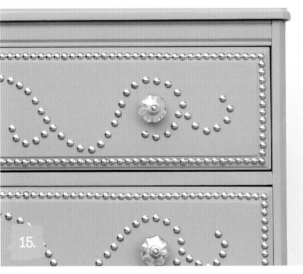

13. Next, add the trim across the top of the drawer in the same way, skipping the holes on the corners. Keep the trim nice and straight.

14. Now lay out the trim to determine the length of the end pieces. You may need to hammer in a few of the loose tacks to fill in any gaps. Finish the trim on both sides and then repeat for the other drawers.

15. Add glamorous new hardware like these mercury glass pulls and let this dresser take the spotlight in your bedroom.

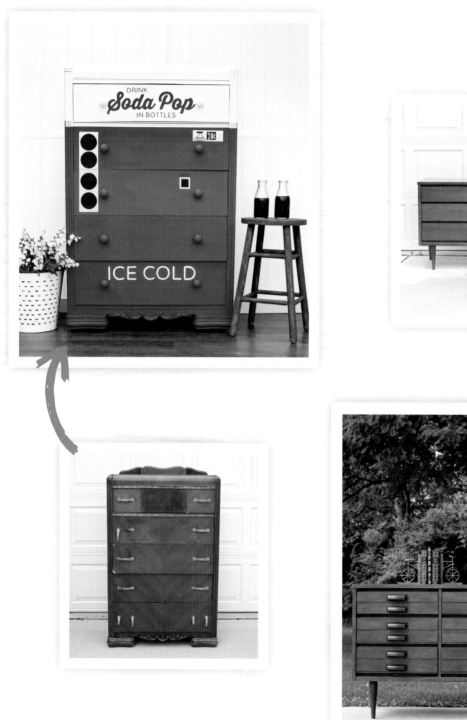

Faux FURNITURE

Faux is the French word for fake, and the pieces in this chapter will fool you into thinking they're something that they're really not. This type of makeover can be the most fun because you can get totally creative and spend a lot of time and attention on little details that are more likely to make someone do a double take and ask "Is that real?"

On my website, Girl in the Garage®, I've shared makeover tutorials for several faux card catalogs, a faux apothecary cabinet and apothecary jars, a painted suitcase nightstand, faux French weathered crates—even how to paint a faux stone finish on a metal planter.

In this chapter, there are three faux furniture makeovers to inspire you. First is a detailed Suitcase Dresser tutorial (page 143), next is a waterfall dresser painted to look like a Vintage Soda Pop Machine (page 147), and finally, learn how to paint a faux stain finish on a Faux Industrial Printer's Cabinet (page 153). Use your imagination— there really is no limit to what you can create with makeover techniques that fool.

Vintage Soda Pop Machine (page 147), Faux Industrial Printer's Cabinet (page 153)

Suitcase Dresser

In this makeover, I'll teach you every step to transform a plain dresser into a stack of charming vintage luggage. It's such a unique project, so why not go all out and have fun with it? Maybe even decoupage some postcards or vintage landmark stickers on the suitcases. I do not recommend using gold hardware with brass screws. I have tried this, and the brass screws break very easily when attempting to screw them in. Save yourself the frustration and stick to silver screws or other hard metals, but avoid brass.

Supplies

Wood filler (I used Elmer's ProBond® wood filler)

Small scraper

220-grit sandpaper

Black or dark gray paint (I used Annie Sloan Chalk Paint® in Graphite)

Paintbrushes

Black furniture wax (I used Annie Sloan's black wax)

Lint-free cloths

Before

Off-white paint (I used Annie Sloan Chalk Paint in Old Ochre)

Jean Marquet Feed Sack with Stripe stencil from Euro Stencil Designs on Etsy (also used in the Armchair with French Grain Sack makeover on page 61)

Taupe paint (I used Annie Sloan Chalk Paint in Coco)

Yardstick

Brown Sharpie

Brown paint (I used Annie Sloan Chalk Paint in Honfleur)

Small detail paintbrush

Pencil

Power driver/drill

3⁄16″ (4.8-mm) size drill bit

Furniture wax (I used Annie Sloan's clear wax)

Leather handle pulls

Light blue paint (I used Annie Sloan Chalk Paint in Duck Egg)

Silver Sharpie

Dark gray paint (I used Annie Sloan Chalk Paint in French Linen)

Black luggage handles

Drawbolt latches in nickel

1″ (2.5-cm) silver screws

Beige paint (I used Annie Sloan Chalk Paint in Country Grey)

Blue paint (I used Annie Sloan Chalk Paint in Napoleonic Blue)

Brown furniture wax (I used Annie Sloan's dark brown wax)

Hammer

Upholstery tacks (I used Woodpile Fun!™ decorative upholstery tacks in antique brass)

Light gray paint (I used Annie Sloan Chalk Paint in Paris Grey)

Black Sharpie

White paint (I used Annie Sloan Chalk Paint in Pure White)

1.

2.

3.

4.

1. Clean the dresser and make any needed repairs. This dresser was pretty solid, and the top just needed to be sanded. Refer to page 182 for helpful tips on making repairs and prepping your piece for a makeover.

2. Remove the drawers and the hardware, filling the holes with wood filler and a scraper and then sanding them smooth.

3. Paint the body of the dresser with three coats of black or dark gray paint.

4. Apply black wax all over the piece with a lint-free cloth. Work in small sections, rubbing it in and making sure you have even coverage. Remember that wax takes about 30 days to fully cure.

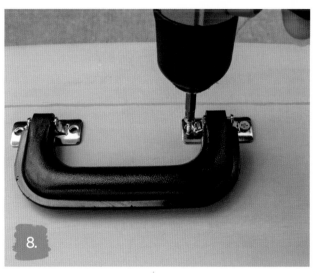

5. Paint the top drawer in off-white. Stencil the grain sack stripes in taupe. Use a yardstick to draw a brown line across with a Sharpie, like where a suitcase would open. Use a small brush to make the line a little thicker with brown paint. Measure, mark, and drill new holes for the leather pulls.

6. Mark off the left and right sides and paint them in brown. Use a small detail brush to make little dashes that look like stitches. Wax the drawer with clear wax. Finally, install the new pulls.

7. Paint the second drawer in light blue. Measure and mark off two strips for "straps" and paint them in off-white (just make sure they're wider than the latches you're going to use). Use a yardstick to draw a line across with a silver Sharpie, and use a small brush to make the line thicker with dark gray paint. Also use this color to make curves at the corners, paint the left and right sides and then paint stitches on the straps. Protect the drawer with clear wax.

8. Install a black luggage handle as a drawer pull and nickel drawbolt latches over the "straps" with 1-inch (2.5-cm) silver screws.

9. Paint the third drawer in beige, and then paint a 1½-inch (4-cm) border around the drawer with brown. Use the grain sack stripe stencil again, but this time with blue paint. Go back and fill in the little space between the outer lines with paint so you're just left with three equal stripes.

10. Use a yardstick and a brown Sharpie to draw a line across the drawer like where a suitcase would open. Make the line thicker with brown paint by using a small detail brush. Wipe brown wax all over the drawer to make it look aged. Hammer brown upholstery tacks around the border. Refer to page 125 for tips on adding tacks.

11. Measure, mark, and drill holes for the leather pull handle.

12. Paint the bottom drawer in light gray. Repeat the steps that you followed to transform the previous drawers: Use black or dark gray paint to make straps, use the feed sack stencil to make stripes, and use a yardstick and black Sharpie to draw a line across the drawer. Paint stitches on the straps with white paint. Wax this drawer with clear wax.

Finally, install a black luggage pull and silver latches over the "straps" with 1-inch (2.5-cm) silver screws.

Vintage Soda Pop Machine

What's more nostalgic than a vintage pop machine? This waterfall dresser desperately needed a new look, and now it's a charming conversation starter in any room. This project uses an overhead projector, painter's tape, and even a Pringles® lid to add graphics that may even fool some people. Discover how to paint your own vintage soda pop machine dresser.

Supplies

Wood filler (I used Elmer's ProBond® wood filler)

Small scraper

220-grit sandpaper

Random orbit sander

Safety glasses and face mask for protection

Primer (I used Zinsser B-I-N® Shellac-Based Primer)

Paintbrush for priming

Paper towels

White paint (I used Annie Sloan Chalk Paint® in Pure White)

Paintbrushes for painting

Measuring stick or tape

Pencil

FrogTape® Delicate Surface painter's tape

Red paint (I used Annie Sloan Chalk Paint in Emperor's Silk)

Silver paint (I used Modern Masters metallic paint in Silver)

Small detail paintbrush

Round shape for tracing (I used a Pringles® lid)

Black Sharpie

Black paint (I used Fusion™ Mineral Paint in Coal Black)

Graphics designed on picmonkey.com

Transparency paper

Overhead projector

Heat-safe surface

Red Sharpie

Silver Sharpie

Furniture wax (I used Annie Sloan's clear wax)

Lint-free cloths

New wood pulls

Before

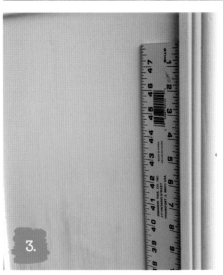

1. Clean and make repairs to your dresser and remove its old hardware. Refer to page 182 for helpful tips on making repairs and prepping your piece for a makeover. I filled the cracks and scratches with wood filler and a scraper, as well as the extra drawer pull holes that I wasn't planning to use. Use 220-grit sandpaper for small areas or an electric sander for big areas to smooth over the wood filler once it's dry.

2. Next, prime the dresser. The Zinsser B-I-N® Shellac-Based Primer that I used tends to be runny, so keep paper towels nearby to wipe any drips. Use wood filler to fill one of the holes on each side of the drawers. Tip: Make a plan for where your graphics will go—and don't let the drawer pulls interfere with the design.

3. Paint the top of the dresser and the top drawer with white paint, going down past the top drawer by a few inches. You may need several coats to get crisp, even coverage. Measure from the ground to the top of the second drawer (in this case the 39-inch [99-cm] line) all along the sides of the sides of the dresser and mark the height with little pencil marks every few inches.

4. Tape across your pencil marks with painter's tape for a straight accurate line.

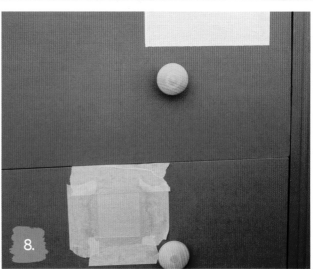

5. Paint everything below the line (including the bottom four drawers) with red paint. Red paint can be fickle like white paint, and you may need several coats for even coverage. Remove the tape before the last coat is dry.

6. Tape off the part of the dresser between the top two drawers, and continue the line on both sides. It will be about 1 inch (2.5 cm) thick. Paint that area with 2 to 3 coats of silver paint. Remove the tape before the paint is dry.

7. Measure a long rectangle on the left side of the dresser and tape it. Make sure the circle that you're going to trace fits within the rectangle. Make it long enough to fit 4 to 6 traced circles, covering 2 to 3 drawers. Paint the area silver, curving the corners just a little.

8. Tape another rectangle on the top right of the second drawer and a square further in on the third drawer. Paint them both silver.

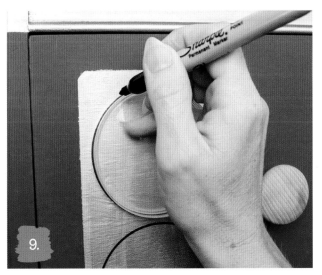

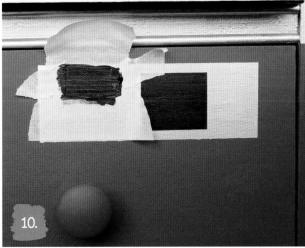

9. Trace the circles onto the left rectangle with a black Sharpie. Then paint inside the circles with black paint.

10. On the silver rectangle on the right side, tape and paint a black square and a thin rectangle for a coin slot. Also paint a black square within the silver square on the third drawer.

11. Design the words for your graphic online. I used picmonkey.com and chose some fonts that I thought looked vintage to type out what I wanted it to say. This really only works for the larger words because the small words were illegible when I made them smaller on the projector.

Save the document to your computer and print it onto transparency paper, then set up the overhead projector on a heat-safe surface. See the Bicycle Armoire project on page 99 to learn more about using an overhead projector for image transfers. Trace the words onto the dresser with a pencil.

12. Trace over the words on the top drawer with a red Sharpie. I don't have the steadiest hand, so this helps me stay in the lines when I paint. Fill in the letters with red paint.

13.

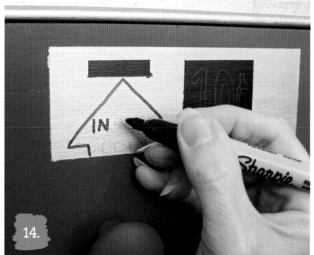

14.

15.

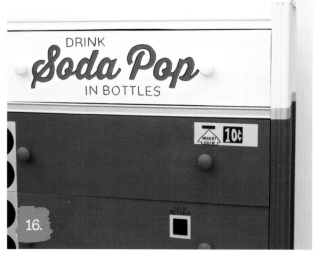

16.

13. As I often do, I changed my mind. (So it's totally fine if you change yours mid-project too!) I outlined the top words with a black Sharpie because I wanted them to stand out a little more.

14. I drew an arrow under the coin slot and wrote the tiny words with a pencil and then went over them with a Sharpie too. I filled in the "10¢" with a silver Sharpie and also used it to touch up any areas where my paint was sloppy.

15. The bottom drawer has "ICE COLD" painted on it—I traced it with a pencil from the projector and then used a tiny paintbrush and white paint.

16. Protect the dresser with clear wax. Use different lint-free cloths for the top (white area) and bottom (red area). Work in small sections at a time, rubbing the wax in and making sure you have even coverage. Be gentle with your piece for the first 30 days or so until the wax has time to fully cure. Lastly, paint plain wooden knobs the same colors as the drawers to blend in more. When you're finished, you'll have a charming vintage soda pop machine dresser to fool your friends!

Faux Industrial Printer's Cabinet

Plain-front dressers are so fun to work on because the makeover possibilities are almost endless! One of my favorite ways to update them is to make them appear to have way more drawers than they really do. Who doesn't love a piece with lots of drawers and vintage-looking industrial hardware?

I really wanted a stained look for this one, but the laminate finish made that impossible. However, I found a pretty simple way to mimic the look of stained wood with just paint and wax. I hope this project inspires you to look beyond a dated laminate finish the next time you're hunting for your next dresser to update.

Supplies

220-grit sandpaper

Yardstick or tape measure

¼" (6-mm)-thin craft wood

Table saw (or have wood cut at the hardware store)

Safety glasses and hearing protection

Super glue (I used E6000)

Clamps

Industrial cup–style drawer pulls

Drill

³⁄₁₆" (4.8-mm)-size drill bit

Screwdriver

Painter's tape

Brown paint (I used Annie Sloan Chalk Paint® in Honfleur)

Paintbrushes

Black or dark gray paint (I used Annie Sloan Chalk Paint in Graphite)

Beige paint (I used Annie Sloan Chalk Paint in Country Grey)

320-grit sandpaper

Lint-free cloths

Brown furniture wax (I used Annie Sloan's dark brown wax)

Black furniture wax (I used Annie Sloan's black wax)

Before

1.

2.

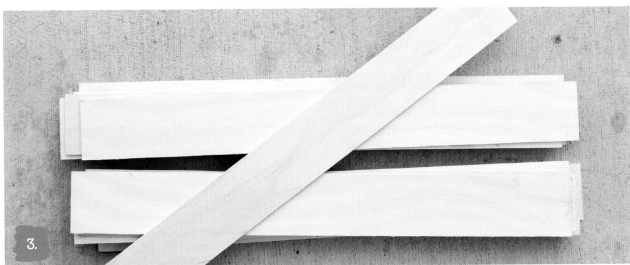

3.

1. Clean and repair the dresser if needed. Thankfully this dresser didn't need any repairs, but I did sand inside the drawers with 220-grit sandpaper because there were some discolored areas and small ink marks. Refer to page 182 for helpful tips on making repairs and prepping your piece for a makeover.

2. Measure the width and height of the drawer fronts. Measure every row because they might not be the same height. In this case, the top row drawers were shallower than the rest.

Determine the size of panels you will need (cut from ¼-inch [6-mm]-thin craft wood) in order to fit two per drawer. You may decide to cut your panels different heights if your rows are different. For this project we cut them all the same size,

and there isn't a very noticeable difference. Also, it helps to have your new drawer pulls when you're measuring, to make sure they'll fit before you start cutting. Plan on leaving a little bit of room above the top panel, below the bottom panel, and a little extra room between the two. The width should be the same width as the drawer. Tip: I have also done several faux card catalogs this way. Instead of cutting long thin rectangles, cut squares and then plan on gluing three per drawer. Search on my website, Girl in the Garage®, to see examples of those makeovers.

3. Since there are 9 drawers on this piece, we cut 18 panels. (Actually, cut one extra to use as a template later.) Sand them smooth on the sides and all around the edges.

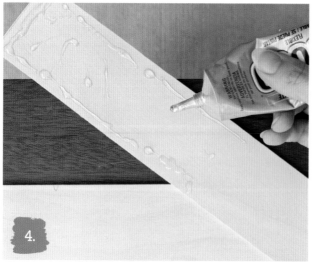

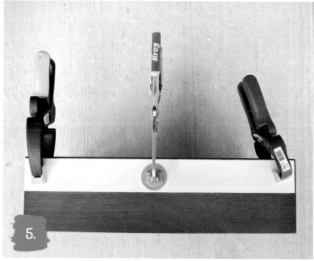

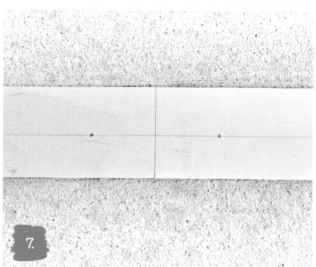

4. Lay the panels in place on the drawer. One at a time, pick one up and apply super glue all over the back of the panel, making sure to cover the corners and edges as well. If you get too close to the edges, some glue may seep out, but you can wipe it away with a paper towel or cut it with an X-Acto knife later if it's already dry.

5. Next, lay your glue-covered side down and secure in place with clamps or anything heavy to make sure the panel stays put. When both panels are glued and clamped, set it aside and start on the next drawer. I recommend letting the glue set for 24 hours before removing the clamps. This step may take a while depending on how many clamps you have!

6. When all the panels are glued and dry, the dresser will look something like this.

7. Take the extra panel you cut and make it into a template for the hardware. Measure and mark the center on each side, and then draw lines across. The point where they intersect is the middle, and then measure out from each side and mark where your screws should go. For example, if the screw holes on the back of the drawer pull are 3 inches (7.5 cm) apart from center to center, then mark 1½ inches (4 cm) on either side of the center point of your template. Drill through the points you marked.

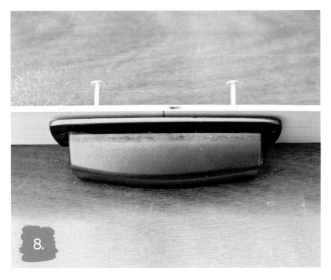

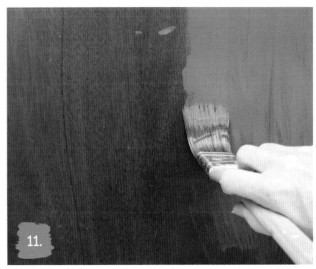

8. Test the accuracy of your holes by screwing your drawer pull into the template. Make sure it looks centered from the front.

9. Place your template over the glued panels and drill through the existing holes all the way through the drawer front. Using this template will save you tons of time and help you avoid mistakes. Repeat for all the drawers.

10. Next, it's time to paint your piece. First, cover the inside of the screw holes with painter's tape to keep any paint from dripping down inside the drawers.

11. To make a faux antique stained look on laminate, start by painting a brown base coat all over the outside of the dresser.

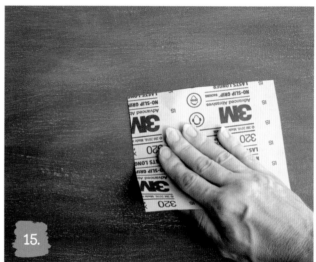

12. Next, dry brush black paint lightly over the brown. Learn more about dry brushing on page 71 of the Dry Brushed French Provincial Nightstand makeover.

13. Then add a layer of dry-brushed beige paint. You're giving your piece more texture and character with every layer of dry brushing.

14. Step back and inspect your paint job. Chances are, there are some areas where you dry brushed a little too heavily. That's totally normal, but you don't want your piece to look like it's been covered in graffiti. Tone down the black and beige by lightly brushing the brown paint back on top.

15. Once you're happy with the finish, gently sand the dresser all over with 320-grit sandpaper. Wipe the dresser clean with a lint-free cloth.

16. Finally you're ready to add a protective topcoat. I wanted an even darker look for this piece so I wiped on brown wax with a lint-free cloth. The left drawer in the photo has no wax; the right drawer has brown wax.

17. Then apply black wax with another lint-free cloth to deepen the hue even more. The left drawer in the photo has only brown wax; the right drawer has both brown and black wax. Remember that wax needs about 30 days to cure before it's safe to regularly use your piece.

18. After all the painted areas have been waxed, install the drawer pulls. What's cool about this style is that it looks like there are four screws from the front, but there are actually just two bolts holding it in place from the back. These pulls were also used in the TV Armoire to Shiplap Storage Shelves on page 175.

19. Here's a closer look at the faux stained wood finish. You can hardly even tell that this used to be a vintage laminate dresser. Now it would look gorgeous in a dining room, entryway, or even as an entertainment center.

Outdated to
UPCYCLED

Once you're confident in repairing and refinishing furniture and adding some creative touches, finally it's time to step a little further out of your comfort zone. This chapter is all about upcycling (aka repurposing) furniture—taking something that was meant for a specific purpose and changing it to now meet a different purpose (as in the Repurposed Hutch to Dollhouse makeover on page 119).

These types of makeovers can be more challenging because they often involve power tools, but don't let that scare you. Many home improvement stores offer classes or one-on-one demonstrations for using tools. Another option is to find a friend to help who's already familiar with the tools, or you can have some of the work (like cutting wood pieces) done for you for free at the hardware store.

Upcycling an outdated piece of furniture saves it from the trash pile, makes it useful again, and makes it something completely one of a kind—and it's almost always guaranteed to save money over buying a brand-new piece of furniture.

In this chapter, you'll learn how to repurpose an antique Singer sewing machine table into a planked desk (page 163), how to upcycle a dated coffee table into an upholstered, tufted bench (page 167), and how to convert an old TV armoire into a storage cabinet with shiplap back (page 175). Use these ideas as inspiration for your own projects whether you're rescuing curbside castaways with your kids in the backseat or thrift-store-hopping on a Saturday morning with your bestie.

Coffee Table to Tufted Bench (page 167), TV Armoire to Shiplap Storage Shelves (page 175)

Singer Sewing Table to Planked Desk

There's just something about old sewing machine tables and their rich history. Once upon a time they were an essential piece in so many homes, but now they're commonly found secondhand because people just don't know what to do with them anymore.

These sewing machine tables are perfect for upcycling into a table or desk. You can preserve the charm and nostalgia of the table while making it more functional for today's modern home. See how easy it is and be inspired for the next time you find a sewing machine table at a yard sale.

Supplies

Screwdriver

Tape measure

1" × 4" (2.5 × 10–cm) pine boards

Chop saw (or have the boards cut at the hardware store)

Safety goggles and face mask for protection

320-grit sandpaper

Hammer

1½" (4-cm) nails

Black paint (I used Fusion™ Mineral Paint in Coal Black)

Paintbrush

Hemp oil (I used natural hemp oil from The Real Milk Paint Co.®)

Lint-free cloth

Before

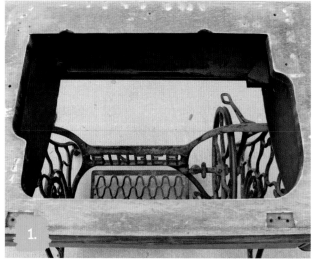

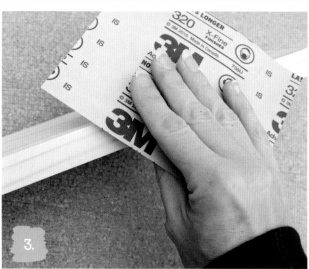

1. First, wipe away decades of dust and cobwebs. Then decide which parts you're going to keep and which you're going to remove.

We removed the sewing machine, the hinged boards from the top of the table, and also the belly, which hid the sewing machine underneath when not in use. As a self-taught seamstress and doll maker, I could never throw the gorgeous sewing machine away! It will be cleaned and put on display in my home.

2. Measure the top of the table. Cut 1 × 4-inch (2.5 × 10-cm) pine boards the same length as the top. If the boards won't fit nicely across the width, plan on cutting the two end boards narrower.

3. Sand the edges and corners of the wood that will be showing on top of the table.

4. If you have an odd number of boards, one will be directly across the center of the table. Lay it in place and hammer it in with three 1½-inch (4-cm) nails near each end. Then attach the boards on one side, pushing each close against the other.

5. Once all the boards are hammered in on the ends, add five nails across the length of the front and back boards near the edge.

6. Paint the metal base and the top of the desk (the planks and the top of the sewing table) black. I used Fusion™ Mineral Paint this time because it's self-leveling and doesn't require a topcoat, which is great since there are tons of nooks and crannies in the metal.

7. Wipe hemp oil over the unpainted wood with a lint-free cloth to revive its finish.

8. Enjoy your custom upcycled Singer planked desk—or use it as a foyer table, as a sideboard, or as a makeup table in your bedroom. It would look amazing in any room!

Coffee Table to Tufted Bench

Have you wondered what to do with all those outdated coffee tables you've seen at thrift stores? Consider transforming one into an upholstered, tufted bench, or ottoman. This type of project may seem intimidating at first, but it's totally doable with a little know-how and patience. And the end result is stunning, for a fraction of the price of buying one new. All you need is a step-by-step plan (and a few power tools) for making it happen. You've learned so much already—I know you can master this project too!

Supplies

Screwdriver

Chop saw (or have wood cut at the hardware store)

Safety glasses and face mask for protection

Work table with clamps to secure your workspace

Kreg Jig® K4 Master System (for drilling pocket holes)

Power driver/drill

³⁄₁₆" (4.8-mm)-size drill bit

Scrap wood

Kreg® pocket hole screws

Table saw (or have wood cut at the hardware store)

Safety glasses and hearing protection

Poly foam pad (I used a 2" [5-cm]-thick pad)

Sharpie

Scissors or electric knife

Yardstick or tape measure

X-Acto knife

Cotton batting (I used Warm & White)

Fabric of choice

Button cover kit

Super glue (I used E6000)

Wax upholstery thread

Long upholstery needle

Staple gun and staples

Hammer

White paint (I used Annie Sloan Chalk Paint® in Pure White and also Old White)

Gray paint (I used Annie Sloan Chalk Paint in Paris Grey)

Paintbrushes

320-grit sandpaper

2" × 2" (5 × 5-cm) furring strip boards (enough for 2 times the length of the bench and 3 times the width)

4 corner braces

Screws

Furniture wax (I used Annie Sloan's clear wax)

Lint-free cloth

Before

1. When planning to repurpose a coffee table into an upholstered bench, always start with a plan. I knew there would have to be some major updates to make sure this would be sturdy and comfortable for someone to sit on.

2. First, flip the table and see what you can keep and what needs to be changed.

3. The top of the table was wider than the base, so it would need to be cut. Also, the legs were going to be changed to a sturdier, more updated style.

4. Remove the frame and legs from the top. This frame had angled cuts because the old legs were tucked behind. But the new legs were going to be attached to the frame directly on the corners.

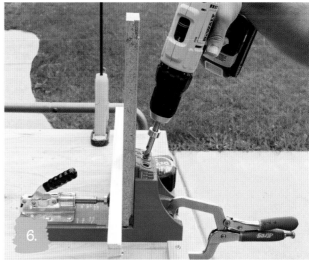

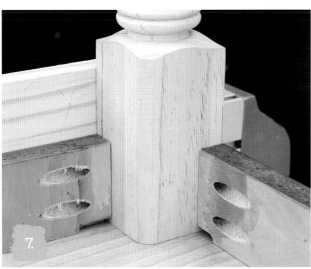

5. The angles were cut off the ends with a chop saw so the edges would be straight across.

6. Next, set up a work table with a Kreg Jig® for making pocket holes. Pocket holes join two pieces of wood together at an angle while hiding the screws. It makes any woodworking project look more professional. Stand a piece of the frame straight up in the Jig and then place a piece of scrap wood behind it for extra stability. Drill into the wood using the Kreg Jig system and make two pocket holes evenly spaced apart. Repeat for each end of each frame piece—but only on the inside (the not-as-pretty side) of the wood.

7. Here you can see the pocket holes for two frame pieces lined up with a new leg. Make sure all three pieces are lined up perfectly, and then use Kreg® pocket hole screws and a drill to join them together. Repeat for all four corners.

8. With that part of the frame finished, you can start working on the top of the bench. Remove any extra trim or hardware from the table's top so you're just left with a plain piece of wood. Cut the piece so it's the same dimensions as the frame.

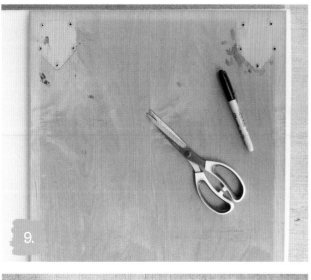

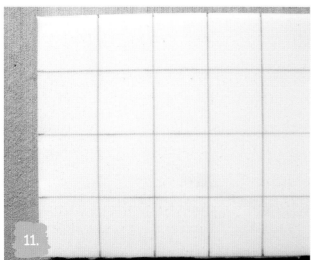

9. Trace onto upholstery foam with a Sharpie. Then cut the foam just slightly larger than the wood. Scissors work fine for 2-inch (5-cm) foam, or you can use an electric knife. The thicker your foam is, the harder it will be to cut with scissors.

10. Measure the dimensions of your foam and determine your spacing for the tufts. I chose to space mine around 4 inches (10 cm) apart, which came to three rows of nine for a total of 27. You totally don't have to do that many—it's up to you how many tufts you want.

11. With a yardstick, draw gridlines to easily mark where the tufts will go at each intersection.

12. Use an X-Acto knife to carve out a little spot where the lines meet. These will help guide you when adding the buttons later.

13. Draw the same lines on the bottom of the bench seat and drill a hole everywhere the tufts will go.

14. Lay out the batting and the fabric and cut them, leaving ample room to fold over the sides of the foam and the wood.

15. Use a button cover kit and make buttons with your fabric. I added a bit of E6000 glue to mine for an extra strong hold.

16. Cut about 14 inches (35.5 cm) of wax upholstery thread and fold it in half. Then slide the folded end through the middle of the button loop.

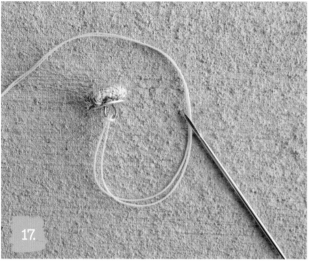

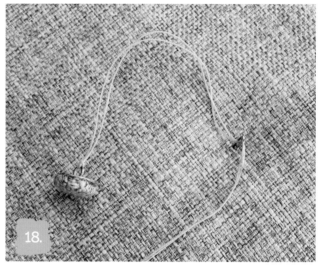

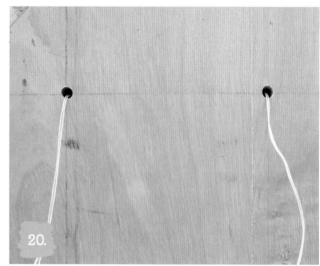

17. Pull the thread ends through the thread loop tightly to make a knot, and then slide a long upholstery needle through the ends about halfway up the thread.

18. Set the bench seat right-side up on top of the frame so you can reach both the top and bottom easily while doing the tufting. Make sure the batting and fabric are centered but not stapled yet. Find one of the drilled holes from underneath and insert the needle straight down through the layers. If needed, you can reach your hand between the layers to guide the needle down through the drilled hole. This is why I recommend not stapling or spraying an adhesive while working on the tufting. Leave the thread hanging underneath for now.

19. Repeat for all the buttons, making sure the creases between them are nice and tight when the thread is pulled from behind. Keep checking to make sure your button lines are straight across in every direction.

20. Stand the bench seat up and lean it against a wall so you can work on the bottom. Your threads will be hanging through like this.

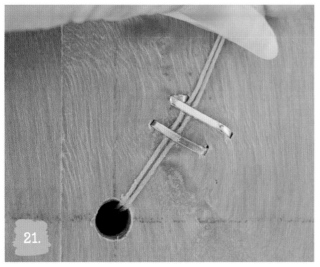

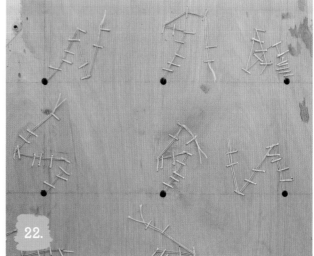

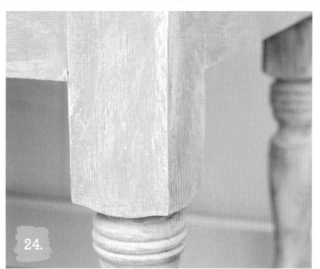

21. Pull the thread tightly and use a staple gun to secure the thread against the wood. Use a hammer also if needed.

22. Add several staples and then fold the thread in another direction. Add more staples and repeat in another direction. This gives the thread more resistance so it won't come loose. It doesn't have to look pretty, it just has to be secure!

23. After each row of buttons is done, tightly pull the fabric and staple it onto the bottom of the seat. Staple all four sides and then do the corners. Learn more about neatly securing the corners in step 4 of the Simple Chair Makeover with Reupholstered Seat on page 49.

24. Paint the bench frame to coordinate with your fabric. I painted mine in Pure White, then dry brushed Paris Grey over it and finally dry brushed Old White on top. Refer to page 71 of the Dry Brushed French Provincial Nightstand project for more details on dry brushing. After the paint is fully dry, (about 30 to 60 minutes, depending on the temperature and humidity), lightly sand the frame with 320-grit sandpaper for a subtle distressed finish.

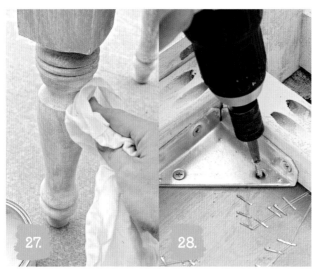

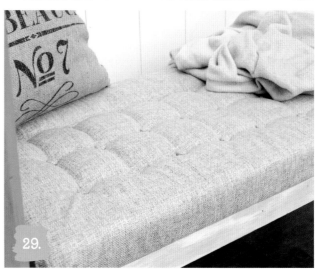

25. Cut furring strip board pieces to use for reinforcing the bench underneath. First, cut two long pieces to fit between the bench legs. Drill two pocket holes at each end and then drill them directly into the bench legs. Then cut three shorter pieces to fit between the two that you just installed. Drill two pocket holes at each end of those also. Drill one board into each end near the legs and drill one directly across the center.

26. Attach a brace in each corner for screwing the bench seat to the frame.

27. You may want to paint over the unfinished wood for a more professional look. Apply clear wax to all the painted wood with a lint-free cloth. Remember that wax takes about 30 days to fully cure.

28. Attach the bench seat to the frame with screws in the corner braces. Make sure they're not too long to poke through the seat.

29. Pat yourself on the back—you've successfully upcycled a thrifted coffee table into a sophisticated tufted bench. I knew you could do it!

TV Armoire to Shiplap Storage Shelves

Old TV armoires are easy to find for a bargain these days; larger TVs and wall mounting kits have made them almost obsolete. But they're fun to repurpose and make useful again! When looking for an armoire to turn into a shelving unit, make sure the sides are thick enough for screws to drill into. I'll also show you how easy it is to upgrade a plain piece like this with shiplap and make it worthy of any country cottage or urban farmhouse.

Supplies

Screwdriver (power or regular)

Tape measure

Table saw (or have wood cut at the hardware store)

Safety glasses and hearing protection

Wood for shelves

Screws

Level

Wood filler (I used Elmer's ProBond® wood filler)

Small scraper

220-grit sandpaper

Primer (I used Zinsser B-I-N® Shellac-Based Primer)

Paintbrush for priming

White paint (I used Annie Sloan Chalk Paint® in Pure White)

Paintbrush for painting

320-grit sandpaper

New drawer pulls

Drill

³⁄₁₆" (4.8-mm)-size drill bit

Hardboard

Hammer

Nails

Shiplap boards (I used pre-primed boards)

Furniture wax (I used Annie Sloan's clear wax)

Wax brush

Lint-free cloth

Before

1. Clean and make any necessary repairs. Refer to page 182 for helpful tips on making repairs and prepping your piece for a makeover. I ended up removing the flower detail from the bottom because I didn't care for it with the new style.

2. Make your plan for the inside. For this project, we planned to remove the doors, all the inside pieces, and the back panel.

3. Use a power driver to make removing hardware faster, but you could also use a regular screwdriver. We saved the doors for an unknown future project—we try not to waste good pieces around here! Also remove the drawer to make it easier to paint and work on.

4. Next, measure and cut pieces for shelves to be installed inside. Cut two shelves that are ¾ inch (2 cm) thick, the same width as the cabinet and about 1 inch (2.5 cm) shorter in depth. I chose to make two shelves because they'll be about 12 inches (30.5 cm) apart, which is a typical distance in many bookshelves. Cut a total of four braces that are about 1 inch (2.5 cm) thick and 2 inches (5 cm) shorter in length than the shelf. Screw two braces onto each shelf, with one end flush with the side and back. The brace is shorter than the shelf because it will look better than seeing a big brace immediately when you walk up to the cabinet.

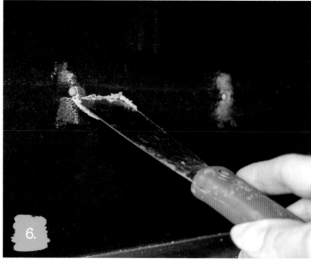

5. When installing the shelves, use a level and get someone to help you. One person can hold the shelf in place while the other puts two screws through the braces into the outer wall.

6. Fill any holes with wood filler and a scraper, let dry, and then sand smooth with 220-grit sandpaper.

7. After your shelves are installed and all repairs are made, you're ready to prime and paint!

8. Prime your piece with at least two coats of shellac primer to avoid bleed-through, especially on cherry furniture like this.

9. Next, apply 2 to 3 coats of white paint as needed and then lightly sand for smoothness with 320-grit sandpaper. Sand a little more around the edges to distress.

10. Make sure your new hardware will fit through the old holes on the drawer. Oops, mine didn't! I filled the old holes and then measured and drilled new ones. Since I had already painted, I had to touch up the areas where wood filler was used.

11. Since the entire back of the cabinet was removed, we had to cut a new piece for behind the drawer. Guy in the Garage cut a piece of hardboard and nailed it into place, lining it up with the bottom shelf.

12. Take your pre-primed shiplap boards (measured to just shorter than the width of the cabinet back—ours were cut by an employee at the home improvement store to save time) and paint them the same white.

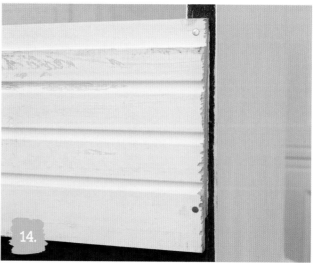

13. Line up the first board so the little notch rests over the top of the hardboard. This will provide a straight line to follow and will make it easier to hold your boards in place while hammering.

14. Hammer one nail into the top and one into the bottom of each end of the shiplap as shown.

15. Take your next board, set the little notch into the groove of the board below it, and nail it just as in the previous step.

16. Continue with the rest of the boards, making sure to keep them lined up straight. Hammer in some extra nails across the very top shiplap board.

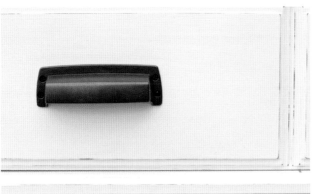

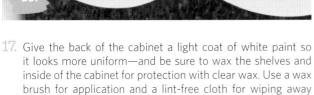

17. Give the back of the cabinet a light coat of white paint so it looks more uniform—and be sure to wax the shelves and inside of the cabinet for protection with clear wax. Use a wax brush for application and a lint-free cloth for wiping away excess wax. Be cautious with your piece for about 30 days until the wax has time to fully cure.

18. The shiplap back gives this TV-armoire-turned-storage-shelves the sweetest modern farmhouse vibe with a low commitment.

19. Antique-inspired iron cup pulls bring the whole piece together beautifully. These pulls were also used in the Faux Industrial Printer's Cabinet on page 153.

Tips for Repairs and Prep

How to Know When to Prime

Priming isn't a must for every furniture painting project, but it is necessary in some cases to achieve a uniform finish:

1. When going from dark or reddish wood to a much lighter color

2. When painting over raw, unfinished wood (unpainted and not sealed)

3. When painting over a very shiny surface

My favorite primer is Zinsser B-I-N® Shellac-Based Primer (with the red label)—it stops bleed-through and helps blocks odors. It does have a strong odor while you're using it though, so work in a well-ventilated area and wear a face mask. You may want to skip primer altogether if you're going for a very distressed finish and want a lot of the original wood to peek through the paint.

Repairing Scratches and Chips

Fill small chips and scratches with wood filler and a small scraper. I prefer Elmer's ProBond® wood filler. For deeper gouges, do several thin layers and sand between each. I have also used wood filler to repair broken table feet like the Dry Brushed French Provincial Nightstand on page 71. Buy stainable wood filler so you can either paint or stain over it.

Tips for Sanding

For very rough or large areas, use an electric random orbit sander. They're fairly inexpensive and get the job done much more quickly than sandpaper alone.

For smaller areas or for careful sanding over finished painted areas, use sandpaper or a sanding block.

Choose the right sandpaper grit based on the surface type and desired outcome. The lower the grit (<200), the more rough the paper will feel—use those for bumpy surfaces. The higher the grit (>300), the less rough the paper will feel—use those for carefully smoothing painted areas and for finishing. Use medium grits (200 to 300) for sanding over wood filler or for distressing furniture.

Dealing with Veneer Issues (Repair or Remove)

For small veneer cracks and chips, use wood filler to fill them. For large chunks of missing veneer, you might just want to remove that layer altogether. Carefully use a scraper to see how easily it comes off. If it doesn't want to budge, lay a damp hot towel over the area for a few hours to loosen the veneer glue and then try again with the scraper. If the wood underneath the veneer is in good condition, sand over it with a random orbit sander and then stain or paint it as usual.

Getting Odors Out of Wood Furniture

Often you can get rid of odors just by applying shellac primer to the surface. You can also try wiping it down with a strong cleaner like TSP. However, if the odors are in drawers and you aren't planning to paint them, set a small bowl of white vinegar inside for a few hours or a few days, depending on how bad the odor is. This is the best option I've found.

How to Repair Drawers That Get Stuck

In very old pieces, the drawers often get stuck and are hard to pull out. There are a few things you can try. If they're really sticking a lot, remove the drawers and sand the edges and sides with a random orbit sander. You can also sand the insides of the dresser where the drawer slides. If they're just not sliding very well, rub candle wax on the tracks and bottoms of the drawers. Finally, you may choose to install drawer guides or tracks inside the dresser if there are none. Even a thin layer of paint can cause a drawer to stick when it didn't before—so if the drawer is a tight fit already, you may want to sand the sides in advance if you plan on painting them.

Thank You

To Scott, aka Guy in the Garage — I cannot imagine life without you. Thank you for helping with projects, for being a constant emotional support, and for not complaining (too much) when our garage and house were overflowing with furniture projects.

To my boys, Xander, Phoenix, and Emerson — Thank you for your encouragement, your patience, and your unconditional love. I am so proud of you guys and the people you're becoming. Keep your creative spirits alive. Mommy loves you so much.

To my mom — Thank you for constantly being on the lookout for new projects, for always believing in me, and for being a loving mother and caring friend. I can never thank you enough for everything you've done.

To my dad — Thank you for always cheering me on and willingly helping whenever I ask.

To my sister — Thank you for helping me start a blog all those years ago even when you probably thought I was already too busy with two wild toddler boys, and for all the quick chats about blogging or just life stuff.

To all my family and friends who have encouraged me to keep painting and chasing my dreams — Thank you from the bottom of my heart.

To all my blogger friends — You girls mean so much to me. You help push me to try new things and be more creative. I'm thankful to be part of this online community.

To Jamie from So Much Better With Age and Amy from Amy Latta Creations — Thank you both for your guidance and encouragement throughout the whole book-writing process.

To all my Girl in the Garage readers — I would not be here without your support and encouragement through the years. Thank you for the comments, the shares, the sweet emails, and . . . everything. I'm honored that you choose to follow my makeover adventures, and I hope that you always feel inspired.

To the ladies at Antiques on Main, Sandpaper, Three Little Birds, Hunt & Gather, Fetching Market, and Yesterday's Treasures — You guys rock. Thank you for everything you've done to support me on this journey.

To Sarah, Lauren, and everyone involved with my book at Page Street Publishing — Thank you for believing in me and for seeing the potential in this book. I'm forever grateful.

About the Author

Jen Crider lives with her husband and three boys in northwestern Indiana, a short drive from Chicago. She's always had a creative side, spending hours in her room working on projects, writing poetry, and teaching herself how to sew as a young girl. She spent several years in the corporate world after getting her MBA but felt overworked and underappreciated. Her creativity had all but dried up.

In 2012, she became a stay-at-home mom to her two young boys. Not one to ever sit still for long, she started buying secondhand furniture and learning how to do repairs and painting during the boys' naptime. Soon after, she started her website Girl in the Garage® to share her projects and inspire other people with their makeovers. Since then, Girl in the Garage has grown to include hundreds of step-by-step tutorials for furniture makeovers and upcycled home décor.

Jen's creative projects have earned her features in print magazines such as *Better Homes and Gardens*, *Romantic Homes* magazine, and *Woman's Day*. She's also been featured in numerous online publications such as This Old House, All You, Better Homes and Gardens, and Country Living.

- Follow Jen's journey at:
girlinthegarage.com

- Instagram: instagram.com/
jen_girlinthegarage

- Facebook: facebook.com/
girlinthegarage

- Pinterest: pinterest.com/
girlinthegarage

- Twitter: twitter.com/
girlinthegarage

- Learn about refinishing and
selling furniture for profit at:
girlinthegarage.com/thinking-
about-painting-and-selling-
furniture

- Discover Jen's upcoming events
and markets at:
girlinthegarage.com/events

- Contact Jen at:
girlinthegarage@outlook.com

Also find her on her other sites:

- DIY Furniture Makeovers:
diyfurnituremakeovers.com

- Thread and Cloth Studio
(handmade dolls, etc.):
girlinthegarage.com/thread-and-
cloth-studio

Index